Footprint Handbook
Cancún & Yucatán Peninsula

RICHARD ARGHIRIS

This is Cancún & Yucatán Peninsula

Once a vast coral reef in a prehistoric ocean, the Yucatán Peninsula now divides the Gulf of Mexico from the Caribbean. Relentlessly flat, its inhospitable interior is consumed by arid scrubland, swamps lagoons and impenetrable jungle.

Yet the Yucatán thrived as a hub of civilization long before the Spanish arrived. Its horizon is broken by the ruins of skyward-reaching pyramids, overgrown temples, fallen palaces and astronomical observatories: sprawling Mayan metropolises where great dynasties once reigned.

None of it would have been possible without the peninsula's network of *cenotes* (sink holes), a subterranean labyrinth of submerged caverns and canyons. The ancient Maya venerated their sacred wells as sources of life and as portals to another dimension.

The Yucatán is a fiercely independent place and can often seem more like an island. It took three brutal campaigns by Francisco de Montejo to 'pacify' the region, and today, scores of rambling old haciendas, sumptuous mansions and religious buildings are testament to the grandeur of the colonial era. But beyond them, in remote rural enclaves, determined Mayan communities stage rituals to honour the ancestral gods of thunder and rain.

Richard Arghiris

Best of Cancún & Yucatán Peninsula

top things to do and see

❶ Playa Norte on Isla Mujeres

Just 13 km across the bay, the 'Island of Women' is a world away from the package tourist hedonism of Cancún. The island's most tempting beach, Playa Norte, with its white coral sand and shallow turquoise water, is a haven for snorkelling, windsurfing or simply relaxing. In summer large groups of whale sharks bask offshore. Page 33.

❷ Palancar Reef off Isla Cozumel

Cozumel was a sleepy place until Jacques Cousteau visited in the 1960s. Since then diving has become a huge part of the island's life. Forming part of the Mesoamerican Barrier Reef, Palancar is a 5-km maze of caves, canyons, overhangs and spectacular subterranean gardens with coral swim-throughs and a wall dropping down to 40 m. Page 51.

❹ Chichén Itzá

One of the greatest Mayan centres of the Yucatán, Chichén Itzá is a rugged place of soaring pyramids, massive temples and intricate carved columns. Looming over them all, the Toltec-influenced El Castillo pyramid attracts thousands of visitors every equinox to witness its light-and-shadow illusion of the serpent climbing the great staircase. Page 95.

❸ El Gran Museo del Mundo Maya, Mérida

A must for those interested in the Yucatán's original inhabitants, this impressive new museum showcases an extensive collection of Mayan artefacts and multimedia displays. From the glories of the past right up to the modern day, the museum takes visitors on an interactive journey with themes as diverse as art, architecture, cosmology and time. Page 77.

5

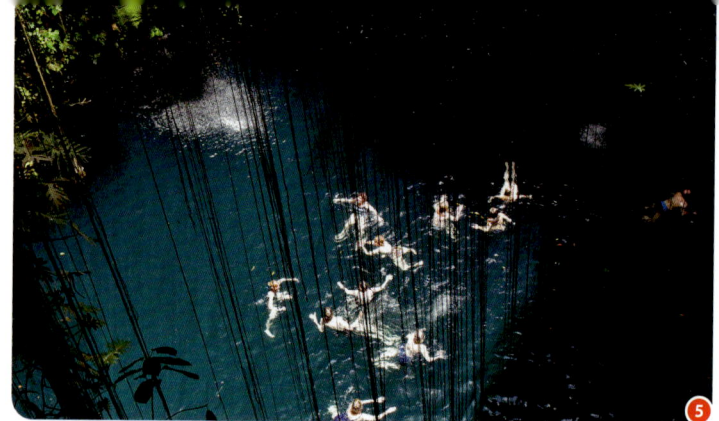

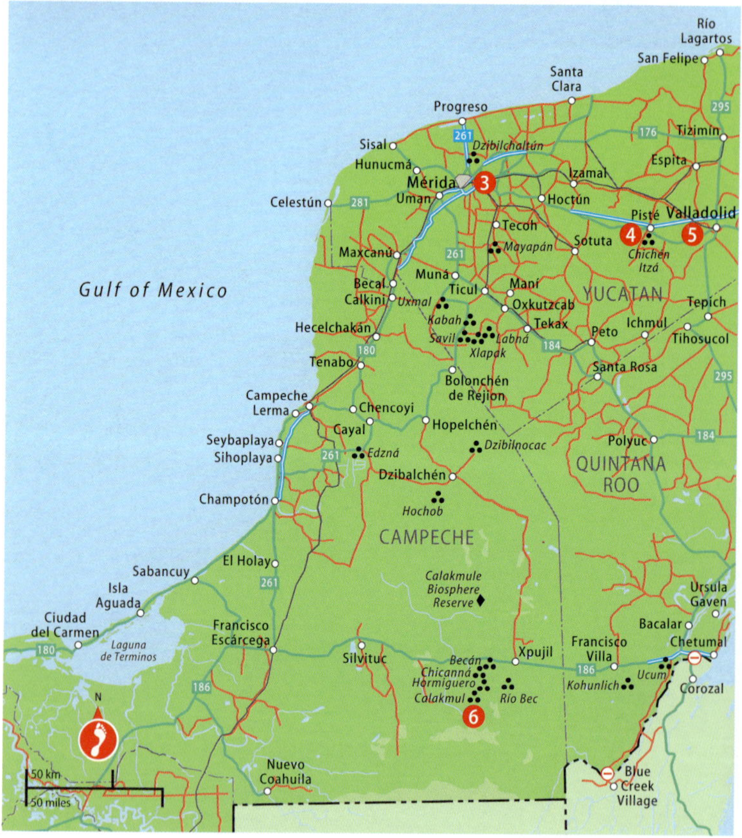
Río Lagartos
San Felipe
Santa Clara
Progreso
295
261
176
Tizimín
Sisal
Dzibilchaltún
Espita
Hunucmá
Izamal
Mérida
3
Celestún
281
Uman
Hoctún
Pisté
Valladolid
Tecoh
4
5
Sotuta
Maxcanú
Mayapán
Chichén Itzá
261
Muná
Becal
Ticul
Maní
YUCATAN
Tepich
Gulf of Mexico
Calkini
Uxmal
Oxkutzcab
Kabah
Tekax
Ichmul
Hecelchakán
Savil
Labná
Peto
Tihosucol
180
Xlapak
184
Tenabo
Santa Rosa
Bolonchén de Rejion
295
Campeche
Lerma
Chencoyi
Cayal
Hopelchén
Seybaplaya
Polyuc
184
Dzibilnocac
Sihoplaya
261
Edzná
QUINTANA ROO
Dzibalchén
Champotón
Hochob
CAMPECHE
El Holay
Sabancuy
261
Calakmule Biosphere Reserve
Isla Aguada
Ursula Gaven
Ciudad del Carmen
Francisco Escárcega
Bacalar
180
Laguna de Terminos
Francisco Villa
Chetumal
Xpujil
Silvituc
Becán
Chicanná
186
Hormiguero
Ucum
186
Kohunlich
Calakmul
Río Bec
Corozal
N
6
50 km
50 miles
Nuevo Coahuila
Blue Creek Village

❺ Cenote Dzitnup near Valladolid

Swimming in a *cenote* is a magical experience. This beautiful underground lake is enclosed by a limestone cavern with stalactite formations and tunnels leading off it, which can be explored by torchlight. The clear mineral-rich water is eerily illuminated and a shaft of sunlight streams in through a hole in the roof. Page 100.

❻ Calakmul

Once home to more than 50,000 people, Calakmul was one of the ancient Maya's most important capitals. The highlight is the huge pyramid of Structure II – thought to be the largest in the Yucatán. The site is surrounded by dense rainforest and you're likely to spot toucans, parrots and howler monkeys jumping about in the canopy as you explore the ruins below. Page 118.

Campeche

Route planner

The Yucatán Peninsula is composed of three neighbouring states. Quintana Roo is the most visited and heavily developed of the three, blessed with sublime Caribbean beaches, tranquil offshore islands and a string of glitzy resort towns, including behemoth Cancún and fun-loving Playa del Carmen. Enclosing the northern Gulf coast, wedge-shaped Yucatán State is the peninsula's bastion of history and learning, home to the vibrant cultural capital of Mérida, a wealth of colonial towns and villages, and mysterious Mayan ruins such as Chichén Itzá, Uxmal and Ek Balam. In the west, Campeche State receives fewer visitors than the rest of the peninsula, but it rewards the curious traveller with an array of stunning archaeological sites and a handsome capital city, very much up and coming.

Suggested itinerary

If time is short, skip Cancún and head to the more relaxed and authentic destinations of Isla Mujeres, Isla Holbox or Tulum, all with decent beaches and plenty of places to sling a hammock. Having chilled for a couple of days, make base in the city of Mérida and explore its fine museums, resplendent architecture and art galleries, before taking trips to see colonial convents and Mayan ruins.

An extra week would be well spent exploring the Sian Ka'an Biosphere Reserve, the colonial town of Valladolid, a few *cenotes* and perhaps one of the peninsula's more remote archaeological sites.

An interesting circular itinerary, three to four weeks, takes you down the coast of Quintana Roo from Cancún to Chetumal, west across the peninsula into Campeche State, then north and east into the Yucatán, and onwards back to Cancún.

When to go

...and when not to

The best time to visit the Yucatán is from October to April when there is virtually no rain, although the mountains can be quite chilly, especially from December to February. The rainy season lasts from May to October but don't be put off by the term 'rainy' – most years, the rains only affect travellers for an hour or two a day. This period is also hurricane season in the Caribbean. Despite the high-profile storm of Hurricane Wilma and a few lesser known local hurricanes and tropical storms, landfall is relatively rare. If a hurricane does arrive while you're in the area you can get details at www.nhc.noaa.gov.

Festivals

If the time and mood is right, there is little to beat a Mexican festival. Fine costumes, loud music, the sounds of firecrackers tipped off with the gentle wafting of specially prepared foods all (normally) with a drink or two. Whether you're seeking the carnival or happen to stumble across a celebration, the events – big or small – are memorable.

August is holiday time for Mexicans and this can make accommodation scarce in the smaller resorts. Carnival (normally the week before Lent), Semana Santa (Easter week), the Christmas holidays, Day of the Dead celebrations (beginning of November) and other important local fiestas are also busy times; book ahead.

Weather Cancún

Month	Temp High	Temp Low	Rainfall
January	27°C	20°C	105mm
February	27°C	20°C	50mm
March	28°C	21°C	46mm
April	29°C	23°C	29mm
May	31°C	24°C	89mm
June	31°C	25°C	141mm
July	32°C	25°C	70mm
August	32°C	25°C	88mm
September	31°C	24°C	184mm
October	30°C	23°C	282mm
November	28°C	22°C	128mm
December	29°C	20°C	70mm

Public holidays throughout the region lead to a complete shut-down in services. There are no banks, government offices and usually no shops open, and often far fewer restaurants and bars. It is worth keeping an eye on the calendar to avoid changing money or trying to make travel arrangements on public holidays. See page 145 for dates.

What to do

from cave diving to sea kayaking

Archaeology

Archaeological sites in the Yucatán run the gamut from a handful of unexcavated mounds to heavily restored citadels with vast pyramids and palatial complexes. Together they chart more than 3000 years of Mayan cultural development; it would be a crime not to visit at least one of them. The sprawling site of **Chichén Itzá** in Yucatán State is the peninsula's most famous and frequented Mayan ruin. Crowned a new 'Wonder of the World' in 2007, one of its pyramids, El Castillo, functions as a calendar, casting serpent shadows on its stairs during the annual equinoxes. Also in Yucatán State, the Puuc civilization reached its zenith at the city of **Uxmal**, the epitome of architectural grandeur. Near Campeche City, **Edzná** has a grand ceremonial centre with giant pyramids, ball court and platforms, all built in Chenes style. Also in Campeche State, **Calakmul** is a very ancient and impressive site dating to the pre-Classic era, a contemporary of the grand metropolis of Tikal in Guatemala, but hard to reach without your own transport or a guide. Running east from Calakmul as far as Chetumal are the so-called **Río Bec** ruins. On the Caribbean coast, **Tulum** peaked during the twilight of Mayan civilization and has a stunning location on a cliff. Inland, **Cobá** is always a favourite for its sprawling jungle setting. Many sites have excellent museums and/or bookshops with detailed booklets and English-speaking guides are usually available at the gates, US$30-45 per group (agree a price before proceeding). At the popular sites, it's best to arrive as early as possible to beat the buses and tour groups.

Beaches

The **Riviera Maya** conforms to ideals of 'paradise' with powdery white-sand beaches, turquoise waters and indolent palm trees, but the crowds in high season are not very heavenly. **Tulum**, where you can bathe in the shadow of a Mayan ruin, has one of the best beaches in Quintana Roo, increasingly deserted as you travel south towards the **Sian Ka'an Biosphere Reserve**. The beaches on the Gulf coast outside **Mérida** aren't quite so stunning, but they are pleasant, intimate and less travelled. **Progreso**, the main port, has a fair beach and a string of low-key fishing villages on the adjacent coastline. In Campeche State, **Seybaplaya** and **Champotón** are popular haunts.

Birdwatching and wildlife observation

In the state of Yucatán, the best places for birdwatching are the **Río Largartos Biosphere Reserve** and the **Celestún Biosphere Reserve**, both home to spectacular colonies of flamingos, along with egrets, herons, ducks, sandpipers and others. Also good for aquatic birds is the **Sian Ka'an Biosphere Reserve**. Offshore, **Isla Contoy** is renowned for its birdlife, as is **Isla Pájaros** near Holbox. The Yucatán's forests, especially in the **Calakmul Biosphere Reserve**, conceal impressive wildlife, including jaguars and tapirs, but these are extremely difficult to spot. Casual strolling at any of the larger ruins is often rewarded with the sight of iguanas sunning themselves on the rocks, scampering agoutis, coatis and other rodents, mot-mots, hawks and occasional monkeys in the trees. Crocodiles are relatively common in the coastal mangroves and have even begun lurking on golf courses in **Cancún** (with unpleasant consequences for one or two golfers).

Caves and cenotes

Essentially a vast, porous limestone platform, the Yucatán Peninsula boasts a very extensive system of subterranean caves. The largest and most famous are the **Loltún caves** in the state of Yucatán, extensively studied for their ancient human and animal remains, and their prehistoric frescoes. The **Calchetok caves** are similarly large with a labyrinth of passages and impressive carbonate sculptures. Near Chichén Itzá, the **Balankanché caves** played an important ceremonial role in the life of the city; the eerie stalactites and stalagmites resemble thrones and ceiba trees. Near Tecoh, outside Mérida, **Tzabnah** has a cathedral-like chamber.

Cenotes are sinkholes; caves with collapsed roofs. Some of these serve as popular local swimming holes, including **Dzitnup** and **Zaci** in Valladolid, but some of the more visually impressive wells are now snorkelling and diving sites (for more information, see box, page 63). Note some underground cavern diving is quite technical and requires special training beyond PADI certification.

Colonial architecture

The peninsula's colonial heritage is concentrated in the states of Yucatán and Campeche. The city of **Mérida**, historically a bastion of Spanish wealth and power, is home to some of the most lavish architecture in Mexico, including numerous ancient churches, convents, monasteries and, on the Paseo Montejo, stunning 19th-century mansions. Many of the city's fine

ON THE ROAD

Shopping

The colourful markets and craft shops are a highlight of any visit to the Yucatán Peninsula. The *artesanía* is an amalgam of ancient and modern designs influenced mainly by the traditional popular art forms of local indigenous communities. Colonial towns such as Mérida are convenient market centres for seeing the superb range of products from functional pots to scary masks hanging over delicately embroidered robes and gleaming lacquered chests.

Weaving and textile design go back a long way and the variety on offer is huge. They can be spun in cotton or wool on the traditional *telar de cintura*, a 'waist loom', or *telar de pie*, a pedal-operated loom introduced by the Spanish. Many woven items are on sale in the markets, from *sarapes* and *morrales* (shoulder bags) to wall-hangings, rugs and bedspreads. Widely available in Mérida, *huipiles* are traditional Yucatec dresses embroidered with colourful flowers, still widely worn by indigenous women. Note the women selling textiles on the streets are mostly from Chiapas, not the Yucatán, but their stock is interesting too. Mérida also specializes in the production of *guayaberas*, smart lightweight shirts that continue to be very popular in Mexico, Cuba and the Philippines. The quintessential souvenir of any trip to the Yucatán, however, is a hammock. Synthetic fibres are often used, so make sure you know what you're getting (see know your hammock, page 31).

---

townhouses have also been converted into luxury accommodation. On the Gulf Coast, steeped in legends of pirates and buccaneers, **Campeche City** boasts a handsome pastel-shaded old town surrounded by fortifications and walls. **Valladolid** has a fine cathedral and ex-convent hidden among its cobblestone streets. **Izamal**, painted entirely in yellow, has a huge colonial convent overlooked by Mayan pyramids. In the 19th century, the Yucatán Peninsula became a global producer of henequen, a type of agave that yields fibres for rope. For a glimpse of the industry at its heyday, the faithfully restored **Hacienda Sotuta de Peón** in Tecoh continues to operate using traditional techniques.

Diving

The Yucatán is a world-class diving destination. The astonishing Mesoamerican Barrier Reef, the 2nd largest reef system in the world, lies off the coast of Quintana Roo, a scintillating expanse of coral skirting the shore from Isla Contoy as far south as Belize. Most serious divers head to **Isla Cozumel**, but there are dive centres at all the major resorts on the Riviera Maya. As ever, the reefs are imperilled by mass tourism, climate change and hurricanes. Near Cancún and Isla Mujeres, don't miss the superb

Museo Subacuático de Arte, an underwater sculpture park.

   Note There are decreasing numbers of small fish – an essential part of the coral lifecycle – in the more easily accessible reefs, including the underwater parks. The coral reefs around the northerly, most touristy cayes are dying, probably as a result of tourism pressures, so do your bit to avoid further damage.

Hiking

The Yucatán is almost entirely flat and the hiking is monotonous compared to other parts of Mexico. It is possible to hike between ruins and *cenotes*, but many of the forests shed their leaves in the dry season and thus offer little respite from the heat. Some of the larger archaeological zones, notably **Cobá** and **Calakmul**, have easy and mostly circuitous trails snaking into the undergrowth, a convenient experience of the jungle with reasonable opportunities for glimpsing fauna.

Kayaking

The coasts of the Yucatán are filled with teeming mangroves and wetlands where you might spot crocodiles, manatees and scores of elegant waterbirds. One of the most popular areas to kayak is the **Sian Ka'an Biosphere Reserve**, where tours can be easily extended to include a visit to *cenotes* and ruins. Inland, the **Laguna de Bacalar** is another fun place for paddling about. Casual sea kayaking is possible at numerous beach destinations with many hotels renting equipment to their guests.

Where to stay

from homestays to hammocks

Hotels and hospedajes

The cheapest places to stay are *casas de huéspedes*, but these are often very basic and dirty. Budget hotels are a gamble that sometimes pays off; always check the amenities and room before accepting. The middle categories are still reasonable value by US and European standards, but high-end hotels have become increasingly expensive as tourism has flourished. Motels and auto-hotels are usually hourly rental, but can make clean and acceptable overnight lodgings for weary drivers.

There is a hotel tax, 10-15% plus 2%, varying according to the state. Check-out time is commonly 1100 but bag storage is commonplace. Rooms are normally charged at a flat rate, so sharing works out cheaper. If single rooms are available they are around 80% the price of a double. A room with a double bed is usually cheaper than one with two singles. A room with three or more sharing is often very economical, even in the mid-price range. Beware of 'helpers' who try to find you a hotel, as prices quoted at the hotel desk rise to give them commission. During peak season (November to April) it may be hard to find a room. The week after Easter is normally a holiday, so prices remain high. Discounts on hotel prices can often be arranged in the low season (May to October), but this is more difficult in the Yucatán.

Price codes

Where to stay
$$$$ over US$150
$$$ US$66-150
$$ US$30-65
$ under US$30

Price of a double room in high season, including taxes.

Restaurants
$$$ over US$12
$$ US$7-12
$ US$6 and under

Prices for a two-course meal for one person, excluding drinks or service charge.

Youth hostels

Hostels can be found in all the major tourist destinations and some of them are excellent. They are not always great value for couples, however, and a shared hotel room is often more comfortable and economical. Both private and International Youth Hostel endorsed accommodation are widely available; the latter offers discounts for members at 22 hostels across Mexico. For more information contact Hostelling **International Mexico** ⓘ *Guatemala 4, Col Centro, Mexico City, T55-5518 1608, www.himexico.com*. Additionally, many towns have a **Villa Deportiva Juvenil**, the Mexican equivalent of a youth hostel, sometimes basic and normally very cheap.

> **Tip...**
> Used toilet paper should be placed in the receptacle provided and not flushed down the pan, even in quite expensive hotels. Failing to do this blocks the pan or drain.

Camping

Most sites are called 'trailer parks', but tents are usually allowed. However, due to their primary role as trailer parks they're often in locations more suited for people with their own transport than people on public transport. **Playas Públicas**, with a blue and white sign of a palm tree, are beaches where camping is allowed. They are usually cheap, sometimes free and some have shelters and basic amenities. You can often camp in or near national parks, although you must speak first with the guards, and usually pay a small fee.

Food & drink

An excellent general rule when looking for somewhere to eat is to ask locally. Most restaurants serve a daily special meal, usually at lunchtime called a *comida corrida* or *comida corriente*, which works out much cheaper and is usually filling and nutritious. Vegetarians should list all the foods they cannot eat; saying '*Soy vegetariano/a*' (I'm a vegetarian) or '*No como carne*' (I don't eat meat) is often not enough. Universally the cheapest place to eat is the local market.

Safety The golden rule is boil it, cook it, peel it or forget it, but if you did that every day, every meal, you'd never eat anywhere. A more practicable rule is that if large numbers of people are eating in a regularly popular place, it's more than likely going to be OK.

Food

Food for most Mexicans represents an integral part of their national identity and much has been written since the 1960s about the evolution of Mexican cooking. Experts suggest that there have been three important developmental stages: first, the combination of the indigenous and the Spanish traditions; later, the influence of other European cuisines, notably the French in the 19th century; and finally the adoption of exotic oriental dishes and fast food from the USA in the 20th century. In 2010, the importance of Mexican food was recognized by its inclusion on the UNESCO Intangible Cultural Heritage List.

Mexican cooking is usually perceived as spicy or hot due to the prolific use of chilli peppers, but equally, maize is a very typical ingredient and has been a staple crop since ancient times. It is mainly consumed in *antojitos* (snacks) and some of the most common are *tacos, quesadillas, flautas, sopes, tostadas, tlacoyos* and *gorditas*, which consist of various shapes and sizes of *tortillas*, with a variety of fillings and usually garnished with a hot sauce. Historically influenced by trade contact with the Caribbean, Europe and the southern United States, Yucatec cuisine is distinctive, and you should not leave without sampling some of its classic dishes. *Poc chuc* is grilled pork in a sour orange marinade. *Pollo pibil* is chicken marinated in sour orange and *achiote*, wrapped and banana leaves and baked; the same dish made with pork is called *cochinita pibil*. A *panucho* is a cooked tortilla with shredded chicken and a salad garnish; *salbutes* are *panuchos* with refried beans inside. *Huevos motuleños* is a breakfast dish consisting of fried eggs on a bed of tortilla and refried beans, all doused in tomato sauce, chopped ham, peas and cheese.

Eating out Meals in Mexico consist of breakfast, a heavy lunch between 1400 and 1500 and a light supper between 1800 and 2000. Costs in modest establishments are US$3-4 for breakfast, US$4-6 for a set lunch, sometimes called *comida corrida*, *menú del día*, or *menú ejecutivo*. Dinner costs are higher, US$7-10 (generally no set menu). A la carte meals at modest establishments cost about US$8-12. A very good meal can be had for US$15-20 at a middle-level establishment, but choose wisely. Street stalls are by far the cheapest – although not always the safest – option. The best value is undoubtedly in small, family-run places. If self-catering, markets are cheaper than supermarkets.

Drink

There are always plenty of non-alcoholic *refrescos* (soft drinks) and mineral water. *Agua* fresca (fresh fruit juices mixed with water or mineral water) and *licuados* (milk shakes) are good and usually safe. Herbal teas, for example chamomile (*manzanilla*) and mint (*hierba buena*), are readily available.

The native alcoholic drinks are *pulque*, made from the fermented juice of the agave plant, tequila and mezcal, both made from distilled agave. Mezcal usually has a *gusano de maguey* (worm) in the bottle, considered to be a particular delicacy but, contrary to popular myth, is not hallucinogenic. National beer is also good with a wide range of light and dark varieties.

Essential Yucatán Peninsula

Getting around

Most destinations on the peninsula are well connected and easy to reach. The exceptions are Isla Holbox, Calakmul and some other ruins in the south, which require extra time and planning. Zipping up and down the coast of Quintana Roo on ADO buses is very easy. Ferries and high-speed *pangas* travel between the mainland and the islands of Holbox, Mujeres and Cozumel, as well as south from Chetumal to the Cayes of Belize.

Best budget places to stay

Hostel Tribu, Isla Holbo, page 41
Posada Los Mapaches, Tulum, page 60
Paakal's Hostel, Chetumal, page 70
Hostel Casa Balche, Campeche, page 110

When to go

The Caribbean coast is inundated with tourists during the summer and winter holiday period. Spring break is notorious for its unfettered hedonism,

Best places to splash out

Mawimbi, Isla Holbox, page 41
Rancho Sak-Ol Libertad, Puerto Morelos, page 45
Rancho Sol Caribe, Sian Ka'an Biosphere Reserve, page 61
Hacienda Xcanatún, Mérida, page 80
Hotel Las Hamacas, Valladolid, page 102

Best restaurants

Labná, Cancún, page 29
Olivia, Isla Mujeres, page 36
La Guaya, Isla Holbox, page 41
Casa Mission, Cozumel, page 53
Mezzanine, Tulum, page 62
Marganzo, Campeche, page 111

especially in Cancún. The region is very hot year round and positively sweltering from April to September. Hurricane season corresponds to the wet season, May to October, with a mini-dry season in July and August. See weather chart on page 10

Best cheap eats

Mercado 28, Cancun, page 29
Babe's, Playa del Carmen, page 47
El Fogón, Playa del Carmen, page 47

Time required

Seven to 10 days is enough for some chill-out time on one of the islands, a trip to Tulúm, a few days in Mérida, and day trips to a ruin or two. Two to three weeks is necessary to see Campeche, rural Yucatán and the lesser visited ruins.

Quintana Roo
State

With its Caribbean shoreline and coral reefs, Quintana Roo is marketed to tourists as the exotic land of the Maya. Amply serviced by the international resorts of Cancún and Playa del Carmen, it is the most visited place in Mexico and, given its natural assets, it's easy to see why: soft white-sand beaches, sapphire blue waters and reclining palms… images of paradise so heavily traded they have become an oversold travel brochure cliché.

Is Quintana Roo a paradise? As a traveller, that depends on you. Some will delight in the region's well-oiled tourist infrastructure; others will want to run away. If so, forgo the resorts and head out to the islands, bastions of low-key tranquility where you can swim, dive, snorkel or eat delicious fresh seafood right on the beach. Or instead, explore the region's intriguing Mayan heritage: the many remnants of ancient Mayan ports and city states, including Tulum.

For some, paradise means getting as far from the crowds as possible, and fortunately Quintana Roo still has many unspoiled pockets: remote wetlands where you might glimpse grazing manatees, tropical rainforests with birds and vociferous howler monkeys, and forgotten Mayan villages where Yucatec is still spoken. If you look beneath the surface, Quintana Roo is far from a travel brochure cliché.

Cancún

a bold, brassy pleasure resort

Love or hate Cancún, its presence on the world tourism market is indisputable. From spring breakers to honeymooners to conference goers to cruise ship passengers, more than three million visitors flock to the city annually. When the Mexican tourist board 'discovered' the place in 1967, it was little more than a tiny fishing village, barren and inaccessible, but blessed with miles of white-sand beaches.

Two decades later, meticulous planning and massive international investment saw Cancún transformed into a city of more than 600,000 inhabitants. Clambering skyward from a sinuous spit of land that flanks the Caribbean Sea on one side, mangrove-fringed lagoons on the other, its high-density Zona Hotelera has become a potent symbol of mass tourism – and all the convenience, sterility and cynicism it brings. For those seeking cloistered protection and 24-hour creature comforts, the amenities are many: high-class shopping malls, international restaurants, gaudy theme parks, rambling golf courses, hedonistic night clubs and a procession of grandiose resort complexes that recall everything from Disney's Cinderella Castle to Nicolae Ceausescu's Palace of the People. By contrast, the city outside is a gritty urban sprawl, down-to-earth and unapologetically real.

The city centre is laid out in street blocks called *manzanas* (M), grouped between major avenues as *supermanzanas* (SM). The precise building is a *lote* (L). Thus a typical address might read, for example, SM24, M6, L3. Streets also have names, often not mentioned in addresses, which can lead to confusion. If lost, look closely at the street signs for the SM/M number. Taxi drivers generally respond better to addresses based on the *manzana* system.

Sights

Cancún Centro, or downtown Cancún, is a world apart from the Zona Hotelera. It evolved from a collection of temporary workers' shacks and is today a massive city with very little character. The main avenue is Tulum, formerly the highway running through the settlement when it was first conceived.

A good place for people-watching and soaking up the local atmosphere is **Parque de las Palapas**, a large plaza with cheap restaurants and wandering street vendors. It comes to life on Sunday evenings, an occasion for live music and dancing, ambling couples, families and children. Nearby, a mildly enthralling 'Zona Rosa' (entertainment district) can be found on **Avenida Yaxchilán**. The city's largest and most visited *artesanía* market is **Mercado 28** ⓘ *0900-1800*, but many prefer the laid-back locals' market, **Mercado 23** (see Shopping, page 30).

If you're based in Cancún Centro, a trip to **Playa Delfines**, the white-sand beach on the eastern flank of the Zona Hotelera, is somewhat obligatory, if not to bathe in the calm Caribbean waters then to behold the panorama of high-rise hotels. On the other side of the spit, **Laguna Nichupté** separates the Zona from the mainland; it is fringed by mangroves, inhabited by crocodiles, a bit smelly and unfit for swimming.

Archaeological sites

There are several very modest archaeological sites in Cancún, recommended only for Maya enthusiasts and those unable to visit any of the larger sites. **El Rey** ⓘ *Blv Kukulcán Km 18, 0800-1700, US$3.25*, inhabited from 1200 AD, was a minor fishing and trade centre and a contemporary of Tulum. The site includes the foundations of two palaces and a pyramidal platform where an extravagant burial chamber was discovered. **El Meco** ⓘ *Carretera Puerto Juárez–Punta Sam, 0800-1700, US$3.25*, was formerly occupied by the Itzas of Chichén Itzá. It features a palace with structural columns and a pyramidal temple with vestiges of serpent iconography; to get there, take a Punta Sam bus from Avenida Tulum (US$0.90) or a taxi (US$3-4).

Where to stay
Alux **3**
Ambiance Suites **9**
Bed and Breakfast Garden **12**
El Rey del Caribe **2**
Hostel Quetzal **14**
Mundo Joven **15**
Suites Gaby **17**
Suites Nader **16**

Restaurants
Du Mexique **1**
El Pescado Ciego **2**
La Habichuela **4**
La Parrilla **13**
La Pastelería **15**
Labná **8**
Los de Pescado **14**
Mercado 28 **16**
Pik Nik **17**

Cancún & Yucatán Peninsula Quintana Roo State • 25

Museo Maya de Cancún
Blv Kukulcán Km 16.5, T998-885 3842, www.inah.gob.mx, Tue-Sun 0900-1800, US$4.50, expository text in Spanish and English, labels mostly Spanish.

Opened in 2012, the Museo Maya showcases a small but compelling collection of archaeological pieces from across southern Mexico. Ceramic gourds, incense burners, carved stone stelae and statuary depicting feathered serpents and shamans are on display, fine examples of Mayan art and its other-worldly motifs. The first exhibition room is dedicated to the state of Quintana Roo and its historical development from early settlement to the Spanish conquest. The second room explores Mayan civilization by theme: culture, agriculture, commerce, science and religious ritual. The third room features temporary exhibits. Outside, the excavated site of San Miguelito is underwhelming, but offers a shady stroll through mangrove forest where you might see an iguana or two.

Museo Subacuático de Arte (MUSA)
www.musacancun.org; costs vary, consult a local tour operator. A typical 2-tank dive from Cancún (4 hrs), US$70-80; snorkel tour (2 hrs), US$50.

One of the world's largest and most thought-provoking underwater art attractions, the MUSA contains more than 500 life-size sculptures, all fixed to the seabed and crafted from material that promotes rapid coral growth. Installations include crowds of people modelled on real persons, a sleeping dog, a piano and a Volkswagen beetle. Inaugurated in 2010, the sculptures are now 'in bloom' and the overall effect is stunning. There are two galleries: **Salón Manchones**, 8 m deep, lies just off the southern tip of Isla Mujeres and should be dived. Off the southern edge of the Zona Hotelera, **Salón Nizuc**, 4 m deep, is suitable only for snorkelling. The stated aim of MUSA is to promote recovery of local reefs and offset the damages caused by climate change, hurricanes and 800,000 tourists to the region annually.

Listings Cancún *map p25*

Tourist information

See also the official Cancún tourism portal, www.cancun.travel, which is a good source of information.

FONATUR tourist office
Av Nader and Cobá, SM5, T998-884 1426, www.fonatur.gob.mx. Mon-Fri 0800-1500.
Flyers, maps, brochures and general information about Cancún and the surrounding attractions.

SEDETUR office
Av Yaxchilán, SM17, T998-881 9000, www.caribemexicano.gob.mx.
Not well located and deals with tourism in the state of Quintana Roo.

Where to stay

By law, beaches in Mexico are public, so you don't have to stay in a pricey seafront resort to enjoy them. Nonetheless, meandering along the strand is not encouraged by some of the larger hotels. Cancún Centro or downtown area has many economical no-frills options, but prices are still higher than other parts of the Yucatán Peninsula. Rates everywhere in Cancún can fall by 25-50% in low season (and double or triple during Christmas and New Year).

Zona Hotelera
Almost all accommodation in the Zona Hotelera – decent or otherwise – starts at around US$100, rises quickly and is best arranged as part of a package holiday. The increased costs, already the highest in Mexico, are partly the result of a government-mandated rebuilding drive after 2 devastating hurricanes, which required all existing hotels to upgrade structures for safety. Just 2 reputable options are:

$$$$ Le Blanc Spa Resort
Blv Kukulcán Km 10, T1800-712-4236, www.leblancsparesort.com.
Sublime, all-inclusive luxury accommodation, complete with first-rate service and spa treatments that promise to take pampering, just like their nightly rates, to a 'transcendent level'.

$$$$ Sun Palace
Blv Kukulcán Km 20, T1-888-414-5538, www.cancunpalaceresorts.com.
A romantic and highly luxurious couples-only resort that's sure to ignite passions. From the same chain as **Le Blanc**.

Cancún Centro
Many downtown hotels, especially the budget ones, tend to be full during Semana Santa, in Jul and over the Dec-Jan holidays. It is best to get a room as early as possible in the morning, or make a reservation if you are returning to Cancún after an overnight trip. Outside the ADO bus terminal, beware 'friendly' and persistent touts looking to make a commission.

$$$ Ambiance Suites
Av Tulum 227, SM20, T998-892 0392, www.ambiancecancun.com.
Immaculately clean, professionally managed business hotel with helpful English-speaking staff, located close to Plaza de las Américas. Rooms and suites are crisply attired with modern furnishings, all in great condition. Amenities include small pool and business centre. Toast and coffee in the morning, welcome cocktail on arrival.

$$$ El Rey del Caribe
Av Uxmal 24 and Nader, SM2, T998-884 2028, www.reycaribe.com.
El Rey del Caribe is an ecologically aware B&B with solar hot water and other green technologies. Its leafy courtyard, complete with small pool and jacuzzi, is tranquil and shady, a quiet place to unwind. Rooms are clean, comfortable and include kitchenettes. Spa treatments are available, including massage. Good for couples and families. An oasis of the calm in the chaos of downtown Cancún.

$$$-$$ Suites Gaby
Av Sunyaxche 46-47, SM25, T998-887 8037, www.suitesgaby.com.
The exterior of **Suites Gaby** is utilitarian and uninspired, but inside you'll find simple, comfortable, recently remodelled rooms with a modern touch. Hot-water showers are strong and the rooms are generally quiet, although the walls are thin. Convenient for Mercado 28 and the restaurants on Yaxchilán.

$$$ Suites Nader
Av Nader 5, SM5, T998-884 1584, www.suitesnadercancun.com.

The rooms at this downtown lodging are just adequate, but the suites are definitely worth a look – all are very comfortable, clean, spacious and quite good value. Each has a fully equipped kitchen and living area, and 2 beds, good for small families with young children. The adjoining restaurant is an excellent breakfast spot and always buzzing with customers.

$$ Alux
Av Uxmal 21, T998-884 0556, www. hotelalux.com.
Conveniently located a block from the ADO bus terminal and a stone's throw from the action on Yaxchilán, **Hotel Alux** has clean, safe, simple, comfortable rooms with a/c, TV, Wi-Fi and hot-water showers; rates include coffee and toast in the morning. Recommended for budget travellers, good rates off season ($). An *alux*, if you were wondering, is a kind of mythical Mayan elf.

$$-$ Bed and Breakfast Garden
Jícama 7, SM25, T998-267 7777, www. bedand breakfastcancun.com.mx.
A cross between a hostel and B&B, this homely, cosy lodging has small dorms ($) and simple rooms ($$), shared kitchen and a comfortable living room with TV and reading material. Located in a quiet, residential part of town, 5 mins from Mercado 28. Surf and yoga lessons available. Breakfast included.

$$-$ Hostel Quetzal
Orquídeas 10, SM22, T998-883 9821, www.quetzal-hostel.com.
Lots of good reports about **Hostel Quetzal**, a fun, sociable place that will suit outgoing backpackers and whippersnappers. Amenities include single- and mixed-sex dorms ($), private rooms ($$), rooftop terrace, bar and garden. Daytime excursions to the local sights are available, as well as legendary nights out to the clubs in the Zona.

$$-$ Mundo Joven
Av Uxmal 25, SM23, T998-271 4740, www. mundojoven.com.
Conveniently located 1 block from the ADO bus terminal, this clean and professionally managed hostel is part of an international franchise. This one has functional dorms ($) and rooms ($$), and a great rooftop terrace complete with bar, barbecue and hedonistic hot tub. Rock on.

Restaurants

The Hotel Zone is lined with expensive restaurants, with every type of international cuisine imaginable, but with a predominance of Tex-Mex and Italian. Restaurants are cheaper in the centre, where the emphasis is on local food.

Cancún Centro

$$$ Du Mexique
Bonampak 109, SM3, T998-884-5919.
Intimate and extravagant fine dining with superb French/Mexican fusion cuisine by Chef Alain Grimond; try the delicious rack of lamb. Courses are served in 3 different areas: sala, dining room and garden. Smart-casual attire and just 7 tables; advance reservations a must.

$$$ La Habichuela
Margaritas 25, SM22, www.lahabichuela. com; a new branch is now open in the Zona Hotelera, Blv Kukulcán Km 12.6 Hotel Zone.
Award-winning restaurant serving delicious Caribbean seafood in a tropical garden setting. Good ambience,

attentive service, Mayan-themed decor and jazz music. Recommended.

$$$ Labná
Margaritas 29, SM22, www.labnaonline.com.
The best in Yucatecan cooking, serving dishes like *poc chuc* and *pollo pibil*. Try the platter and sample a wide range of this fascinating regional cuisine. Good lunchtime buffet (**$$**). Highly recommended.

$$$ La Parrilla
Yaxchilán 51, SM22, www.laparrilla.com.mx.
A buzzing, lively joint, always busy and popular, especially with Mexican families. They serve mouth-watering grill platters, ribs, steaks and other carnivorous fare. Try the enormous margaritas in exotic flavours – hibiscus flower and tamarind.

$$$-$$ El Pescado Ciego
Av Nader esquina Rubia, SM3. Closed Thu and Sun.
Low-key and relaxed, a good place for friends and lovers, **El Pescado Ciego** serves flavourful contemporary seafood dishes with a Mexican twist. Offerings include tasty shrimp tacos, lobster quesadillas, tuna steaks and filleted catch of the day.

$$ Pik Nik
Calle Tulipanes, SM22.
A fun, local, friendly place to kick back and gorge on hearty Mexican food and drink. Expect the usual staples, including tacos, burritos and quesadillas, as well as Mexican beers and cocktails. Good service, a great place for groups, with terraced seating on a pedestrian street near Plaza del las Palapas.

$ Los de Pescado
Av Tulum 32, SM20, www.losdepescado.com. Lunch and early supper only.
Excellent Baja California-style fish burritos and tacos, prawn ceviche, beer, soda and absolutely nothing else. Charmless setting and service, but great fast food. Recommended.

$ Mercado 28
SM28. Open for lunch and early supper.
The half dozen or so kitchens nestled inside in the *artesanía* market serve the best budget meals in the city; **Mi Rancho** is one of the better ones. Set meals include generous Mexican staples and specialities, such as *pollo con mole poblano* (chicken in chocolate and chilli sauce). Most come with a soup starter, tortillas, nachos, salsa and a drink, all for US$5. If the waiter hands you the more expensive à la carte menu, insist on *comida del día*. Wandering mariachis may serenade you. Recommended.

Cafés

La Pastelería
Av Cobá and Guanábana, SM25.
La Pastelería, formerly known as **La Crepería**, is a European-style café-patisserie serving aromatic coffee and a host of elegant desserts, including sumptuous cakes and pastries adorned with lashings of rich, dark Mexican chocolate.

Bars and clubs

Cancún is famous for its debauched nightlife. Clubs are mostly concentrated at Blv Kukulcán Km 9 in the Zona Hotelera. All tastes are catered to, but most of the action gravitates to chic lounge bars and enormous discos, invariably packed to the rafters with revellers during spring break.

Establishments come and go with the seasons, but one that has withstood the test of time is **Coco Bongo**, www.cocobongo.com.mx, famous for its vivid dance and acrobatic displays. Some tour agencies offer 'club crawl' excursions, allowing you to sample a few different places in one evening, a good option for groups; try **Party Rockers Cancún**, T998-883-0981, www.partyrockerscancun.com. Downtown, you'll find comparatively low-key bars and pubs in the Zona Rosa on Av Yaxchilán.

Shopping

There are several shopping malls in the Zona Hotelera. The main one is **Kukulcán Plaza**, Blv Kukulcán Km 13, www.kukulcanplaza.com, with more than 170 retail outlets. There are others, including **La Isla**, Blv Kukulcán Km 12.5, mostly catering to the luxury shopper. Downtown, the big *artesanía* market is **Mercado 28**, where you'll find a plethora of handmade items including silver jewellery from Taxco, hammocks from Mérida, ceramic Mayan figurines, cowboy boots, sombreros, masks, sarapes, t-shirts and more; the quality of production varies. Note prices are hiked to the limit and the salesmen are mean and aggressive. Whatever happens, smile politely and bargain hard; most vendors expect to get at least half what they originally asked. Due to credit card rip-offs, it is safer to pay cash only. You could also try the locals' market, **Mercado 23**, at the end of Calle Cedro, off Av Tulum. It's a bit tatty and tacky, but has cheaper souvenirs and friendlier salesmen. For an American-style mall experience in Cancún Centro, your best option is **Plaza de las Américas** on Av Tulum.

What to do

From booze cruises to canopy tours, parasailing to paintballing, the array of activities on offer in Cancún is vast. The listings below highlight some of the more interesting options, but are in no way exhaustive. Consult your hotel or the tourist information office for more possibilities.

Cooking
Can Cook in Cancún, *T998-147 4827, www.cancookincancun.com*. A master of Mexican cuisine, chef Claudia has been in kitchens all her life. Classes are fun and intimate, take place in Claudia's home and include an overview of traditions and regional specialities, as well as practical instruction in ingredients and flavours.

Diving and snorkelling
See box, page 63, for information on cave diving.
Scuba Cancun, *Kukulcán Km 5, T998-849 7508, www.scubacancun.com.mx*. A medium-sized dive centre run by Captain Luis Hurtado who has more than 3 decades' diving experience. He offers a range of sea, cavern and *cenote* dives, including trips to the MUSA, snorkelling tours and accelerated PADI courses.

Sports cars
Exotic rides, *Carretera Cancún Airport Km 7.5, T998-882 0558, www.exoticridescancun.com*. Experience the speed, power and performance of Ferrari, Lamborghini and other 'exotic' sports cars. Training and test driving takes place at a private race track.

ON THE ROAD
Know your hammock

Different materials are available for hammocks. Some you might find include sisal, which is very strong, light, hard-wearing but rather scratchy and uncomfortable, and is identified by its distinctive smell; cotton, which is soft, flexible, comfortable, not as hard-wearing but, with care, is good for four or five years of everyday use. It is not possible to weave cotton and sisal together, although you may be told otherwise, so mixtures are unavailable. Cotton/silk mixtures are offered, but will probably be an artificial silk. Nylon is very strong and light but it's hot in hot weather and cold in cold weather.

Never buy your first hammock from a street vendor and never accept a packaged hammock without checking the size and quality. The surest way to judge a good hammock is by weight: 1.5 kg (3.3 lb) is a fine item, under 1 kg (2.2 lb) is junk (advises Alan Handleman, a US expert). Also, the finer and thinner the strands of material, the more strands there will be, and the more comfortable the hammock. The best hammocks are the so-called 3-ply, but they are difficult to find. There are three sizes: single (sometimes called *doble*), *matrimonial* and family (buy a *matrimonial* at least for comfort). If judging by end-strings, 50 would be sufficient for a child, 150 would suit a medium-sized adult, 250 a couple. Prices vary considerably so shop around and bargain hard.

Surfing
360 Surf school, *Blv Kukulcán Km 9.5, opposite Señor Frog, T998-241 6443, www.360surfschoolcancun.com*. The waves in Cancún are relatively gentle, making it a great place to learn how to surf. Managed by David '360Dave' Wanamaker, **360 Surf School** has been getting beginners up onto boards for more than 14 years. You'll surf, or your money back.

Tour operators
Ecocolors, *Calle Camarón 32, SM27, T998-884 3667, www.ecotravelmexico.com*. Socially responsible and environmentally aware tours of the Yucatán Peninsula and beyond. Specialities include biking, birdwatching, hiking and wildlife photography.

Transport

Air
The airport is 16 km south of the city. Shared fixed-price shuttles to the **Zona Hotelera** or the centre depart hourly Mon-Fri 0800-2000, US$12; pay at the kiosk outside airport. Private taxis are US$45 one way, US$70 round trip. Be sure to know the name and address of your hotel, or the driver may offer to take you to a lodging of their own choice.

Cancún airport (**CUN**), *Carretera Cancún–Chetumal Km 22, T998-848 7200, www.cancun-airport.com*, has expensive shops, restaurants, currency exchange, car rental, hotel reservation agencies and ATMs. Terminal 1 serves domestic airlines; Terminal 2 and Terminal 3 serve international airlines. ADO buses go from the airport to **Cancún Centro**, every 30 mins, ½ hr, US$4; **Puerto Morelos**, every 30-40 mins, ½ hr, US$6, and **Playa del Carmen**, every 30-40 mins, 1½ hrs, US$10.

Bus

Local Ruta 1 and Ruta 2 buses travel between Cancún Centro (downtown) and the Zona Hotelera, US$0.70. Ruta 1 runs 24 hrs and follows Av Tulum, the city's principal thoroughfare. Ruta 2 runs 0500-0330 and goes via Av Cobá. Shuttle buses to **Puerto Juárez** for the ferry to Isla Mujeres follow Av Tulum, US$0.65, opposite side to the bus station.

Long distance Cancún's **ADO** bus terminal, C Pino, SM23, at the junction of Av Tulum and Uxmal, is a hub for routes west to Mérida and south to Tulum and beyond to Chetumal, open 24 hrs, left luggage, rates vary depending on size, open 0600-2200. Rapid ticket booths for the airport and Playa del Carmen.

To **Cancún Airport**, every 30 mins, ½ hr, US$4. To **Chetumal**, frequent departures, 6 hrs, US$27. To **Chichén Itzá**; all 2nd-class buses to Mérida stop here, fewer 1st-class buses, 4 hrs, US$14. To **Mérida**, frequent departures, 4½ hrs, US$25. To **Palenque**, 1st class, 1545, 2030, 12½ hrs, US$62; and an ADO GL, 1745, 13 hrs, US$68. To **Playa del Carmen**, every 10 mins, 1½ hrs, US$4. To **Puerto Morelos**, frequent departures, 30 mins, US$2.30. To **San Cristóbal**, OCC, 1545, 2030 18 hrs, US$69, **ADO GL**, 1745, US$83. To **Tulum**, ADO, frequent departures, 2½ hrs, US$9, and many cheaper 2nd-class buses. To **Valladolid**, frequent departures, 2½ hrs, US$12.50. To **Villahermosa**, 1st class, many departures, 13 hrs, US$62. **Expreso de Oriente** also has services to the more obscure destinations of **Tizimín** (3 hrs, US$10), **Izamal**, **Cenotillo** and **Chiquilá**.

Car

Car hire There are many car hire agencies, including **Dollar**, **Hertz**, **Thrifty**, **Budget** and others, with offices on Av Tulum, in the Hotel Zone and at the airport; look out for special deals, but check vehicles carefully.

Car parking Do not leave cars parked in side streets; there is a high risk of theft. Use the car park on Av Uxmal.

Ferry

For ferries to **Isla Mujeres**, regular *combis* and buses travel along Av Tulum en route to **Puerto Juárez** (marked Pto Juárez or Punta Sam), US$0.80, where services to the island depart from the **Ultra Mar** terminal, T998-843 2011, www.granpuerto.com.mx, at Gran Puerto (recommended), every 30 mins, 0500-2330, US$5.50, children US$3.50; and from the **Magaña Express** terminal, T998 877 0618, 2 blocks north of Ultra Mar, hourly, 0800-2000. **Ultra Mar** services also depart from the Zona Hotelera (Playa Caracol, Playa Tortugas and El Embarcadero), every 1-2 hrs, US$11. Car ferries depart 4-5 times daily from **Punta Sam**, north of Puerto Juárez on the coast, US$20 for a car and driver, US$1.50 for each additional passenger.

Taxi

Taxis are abundant in Cancún. Fares are based on a zone system and most short journeys downtown cost US$2. Overcharging is common; avoid taxis waiting outside hotels or restaurants.

Isla Mujeres

a refreshing antidote to the urban sprawl of Cancún

★Blending Caribbean and Mexican styles, and more than faintly recalling the Mediterranean too, Isla Mujeres (Women Island) is a place to unwind, unravel and forget about the hurly burly of package tourism. In pre-Hispanic times, the island served as a shrine to Ixchel, the Mayan goddess of childbirth, traditionally associated with midwifery, fertility, femininity and the moon. It received its current name after Spanish conquistadors came ashore in the 16th century and discovered scores of clay idols depicting the goddess and her daughters: Ixchebeliax, Ixhunie and Ixhunieta.

Blessed with one of the finest beaches in Mexico, kaleidoscopic coral reefs and, of course, an appropriately alluring name, Isla Mujeres has been a popular tourist destination since the 1960s. Unlike its younger sibling on the mainland, Cancún, it has endured remarkably well; even with the pressure of big dollars on its doorstep, it remains defiantly low-key, a sanctuary for travellers everywhere. The magic begins after dusk, once the day-trippers have gone.

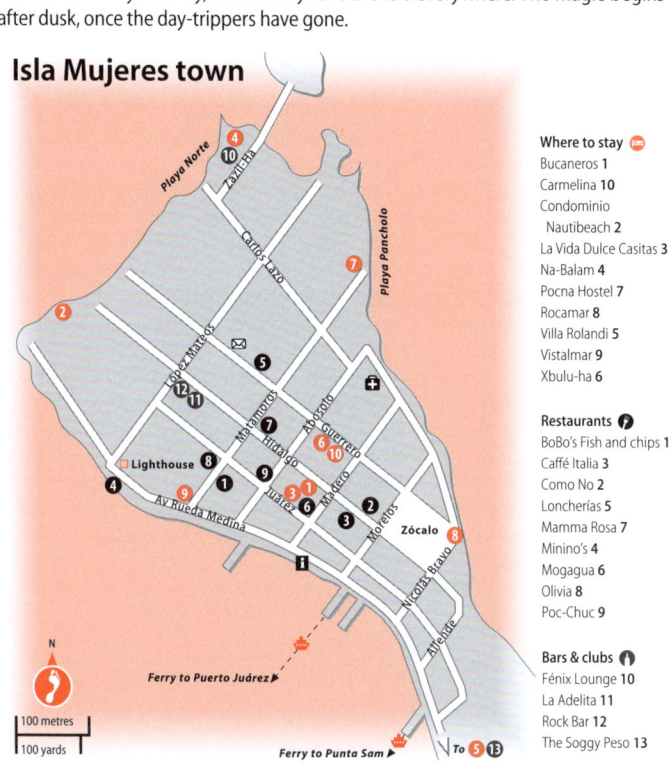

Isla Mujeres town

Where to stay
Bucaneros 1
Carmelina 10
Condominio Nautibeach 2
La Vida Dulce Casitas 3
Na-Balam 4
Pocna Hostel 7
Rocamar 8
Villa Rolandi 5
Vistalmar 9
Xbulu-ha 6

Restaurants
BoBo's Fish and chips 1
Caffé Italia 3
Como No 2
Loncherías 5
Mamma Rosa 7
Minino's 4
Mogagua 6
Olivia 8
Poc-Chuc 9

Bars & clubs
Fénix Lounge 10
La Adelita 11
Rock Bar 12
The Soggy Peso 13

Sights

An unkempt seasonal refuge for pirates and fishermen, Isla Mujeres was largely uninhabited in the colonial era. It saw significant settlement only in 19th century when the violence and persecution of the Caste War drove scores of refugees to its shores. Today, tourism has all but replaced fishing as the mainstay of the local economy. Fortunately, **Isla Mujeres Town** remains strictly low-rise and unobtrusive, its colourful grid of streets boasting scores of intimate little restaurants, bars, cafés and *artesanía* shops. The island is 7 km long and 650 m wide. The town, at the northern end, can be easily covered on foot. For explorations further afield, hire a golf cart, moped or bicycle, or take the bus. The best beach on the island, **Playa Norte**, is conveniently located on the fringe of the action.

Heading south from the town, the main seafront artery, **Avenida Rueda Medina**, becomes the **Carretera Garrafón** and skirts the airport, marinas and a series brackish lagoons which the ancient Maya harvested for their salt. Inland, near the southern tip of Laguna Makax, the ruined **Hacienda Mundaca** ⓘ *0900-1700, US$2.50*, was constructed in 1860 on the site of a Mayan temple. Originally called 'Vista Alegre', its owner, a notorious Spanish slave trader, Fermín Antonio Mundaca, fell madly in love with a local girl, Martiniana (Prisca) Pantoja, but she rejected him for a younger lover. Mundaca eventually went insane, dying alone in the city of Mérida on the mainland. His tomb on Isla Mujeres remains empty, but its bitter epitaph was carved by his own hand: "As you were, so was I. As I am, so you will be."

For something a bit lighter, the **Capitán Dulché Beach Club** ⓘ *Cra Garrafon Km 4, T998-849 7594, www.capitandulche.com, daily 1030-1930*, is a new addition to the island, complete with sun loungers, bar, restaurant and a small museum of maritime artefacts, historic photos and handsome model ships. To the northwest, the **Carretera Sac Bajo** doubles back on a narrow spit, passing between the Caribbean sea and the shores of Laguna Makax. The government-sponsored **Tortugranja** ⓘ *Cra Sac Bajo Km 5, daily 0900-1700, US$2.50*, is a small turtle hatchery with fish-filled aquariums and young turtles at different stages of development; knowledgeable staff explain their life cycles and migratory habits.

At the southern end of the island, the **Garrafón Natural Reef Park** ⓘ *Cra Garrafón, Km 6, T01-866-393 5158, www.garrafon.com*, is a luxury adventure resort offering snorkelling, kayaking, zip-lining and bike tours; packages from US$59. Nearby, the **Santuario a la Diosa Ixchel** ⓘ *daily 0900-1700, US$2.50*, is a crumbling ruin of a temple dedicated to Ixchel. The structure has been sadly damaged by hurricanes, but nonetheless commands a potent position on cliffs above the crashing ocean (take care on the slippery paths). If you can get there, it is a magical place to experience the sunrise.

Listings Isla Mujeres *map p33*

Tourist information

The official online information portal is www.isla-mujeres.com.mx.

Tourist office

Av Rueda Medina 130, T998-877 0767.
Located on the seafront opposite the ferry terminals, the tourist office has maps, flyers and helpful staff, some of whom speak English.

Where to stay

$$$$ Condominio Nautibeach
Playa Los Cocos, T998-877 0606, www.nautibeach.com.
Condominio Nautibeach boasts an enviable setting on Playa Norte, undoubtedly the best beach on the island. The hotel is vast and its accommodations include rooms, studios and apartments, all comfortable and predictably well appointed. Pool and restaurant are among the amenities, perfectly placed to admire the sunset.

$$$$ Hotel Villa Rolandi
Cra Sac-Bajo, T998-999 2000, www.villarolandi.com.
A large, popular, award-winning 5-star luxury beach resort with astonishing ocean views. Suites are very comfortable, adorned in Italian marble and boast jacuzzi terraces. General amenities include 2 pools, 'private' beach, spa services, bar-restaurant and, at extra cost, a private yacht. No children under 13.

$$$$-$$$ Na Balam
Zazil Ha 118, T998-881 4770, www.nabalam.com.
Overlooking blissful Playa Norte, **Na Balam** is a boutique yoga and spa resort with 35 rooms and suites, 2 restaurants, pool and jacuzzi. Daily yoga classes include relaxation, pranayama, asana, chanting and meditation; retreats and packages available.

$$$ La Vida Dulce Casitas
Juárez 13, T515-974 6777, www.islatrip.com.
A lot of love has gone into this *hotelito*, a very popular lodging that will suit couples or small families. Managed by attentive and hospitable hosts, Steve and Jerri, they offer 3 comfortable, cosy apartments that sleep 3-4. Book in advance.

$$$ Rocamar
Nicolás Bravo and Zona Marítima, T998-877 0101, www.rocamar-hotel.com.
Crisp and minimalist, the **Rocamar** is an island favourite, now more than 30 years old. Its rooms and suites are clean and unfussy; the best of them enjoy expansive views of the Caribbean sea and sunrise. Note the **Rocamar** is located on the quieter, eastern side of the island, where swimming is not recommended.

$$$-$$ Xbulu-ha
Guerrero 4, T998-877 1783, www.sites.google.com/site/hotelxbuluha.
A very clean, cosy and unpretentious hotel with simple but comfortable rooms, all equipped with fridges, a/c and microwave. The suites are best and have kitchenettes (**$$$**). Quiet, friendly and good value. Recommended. The name means 'bubbling water' in Yucatec Maya.

$$ Hotel Bucaneros
Hidalgo 11, T998-877 1228, www.bucaneros.com.

Located right in the heart of town, **Hotel Bucaneros** is a pleasant, well-established, professionally managed hotel. It has a variety of modern rooms and suites, all with calm, neutral interiors; some have balconies and views.

$$-$ Vistalmar
Av Rueda Medina on promenade, T998-877 0209.
Popular with Canadian and American retirees, who stay long-term during the northern winter. The friendly **Vistalmar** has a range of reasonable rooms, some better equipped than others. Ask for one on the top floor, where you will enjoy sea breezes. Better to reserve in advance Jan-May. $ for longer stays.

$ Hotel Carmelina
Guerrero 4, T998-877 0006, hotel_carmelina@hotmail.com.
Locally owned motel-style place with parking. The rooms are simple, sparse and clean, all with a/c, Wi-Fi and hot water, some with fridge. Good value, recommended for budget travellers.

$ Pocna Hostel
Top end of Matamoros on the northeast coast, T998-877 0090, www.pocna.com.
An island institution, popular with backpackers, but not beloved by all. Grounds are large and warren-like with scores of scruffy dorms and rooms, as well as a campground. There's internet access, lounge and beach bar, dive shop, bike rental, spa services, free activities like yoga and drumming, and DJs and live music in the evenings, often continuing until 0300. Book in advance in high season. Price per person.

Restaurants

$$$ Olivia
Av Matamoros between Juárez and Medina, www.olivia-isla-mujeres.com. Dinner only, closed Mon except Jan-Mar.
Founded by an Israeli couple, Lior and Yaron, **Olivia** serves fabulous Mediterranean home cooking, including old family recipes, and Greek, Moroccan and Middle Eastern specialities, such as kebabs, home-baked breads and sweet baklava. A great spot for a romantic meal. Recommended.

$$$-$$ Como No
Hidalgo 7, www.isla mujeresdining.com.
A popular rooftop restaurant-bar that serves tasty Mediterranean food alongside eclectic international dishes including schnitzel, tapas and Thai curry. The mojitos are particularly delicious and highly recommended. A joint venture with **The Patio**, downstairs, also good.

$$$-$$ Mamma Rosa
Hidalgo and Matamoros.
A well-attired and authentic Italian restaurant with a relaxed, romantic ambiance. They serve good pasta, pizzas and seafood, with a fine selection of Italian wines. Personable service with dining inside or al fresco.

$$ BoBo's Fish and Chips
Av Matamoros 14A.
A casual little joint with a few seats on the street outside. They serve wholesome beer-battered fish, burgers, chicken wings, chips and cheap beer; comfort food for weary travellers. Owner Brian is friendly and talkative, tending bar as he serves.

$$ Minino's
Av Rueda Medina.
One of the best seafood restaurants in town, unpretentious, scruffy and often recommended by the locals. They offer delicious fresh fish fillets, squid, octopus, ceviche and lobster. Dining is on the sand at plastic tables. Good place, good food.

$$ Mogagua
Av Juárez and Madero.
Closely resembling a North American coffeeshop, **Mogagua** has a laid-back, arty vibe. They serve good coffee from Chiapas (try the iced frappés), Spanish tapas and other international fare, and in the evening, sangria. A sociable place for breakfast before hitting the beach. Good, friendly service. Recommended.

$$-$ Caffé Italia
Av Hidalgo between Morelos and Madero.
A cute little eatery serving breakfast, lunch and light snacks. Offerings include sweet and sour crêpes ($), fresh fruit juices, excellent strong coffee and authentic Italian home-cooking, including pizzas and pasta. Friendly, hospitable owner.

$ Loncherías
Northwest end of Guerrero, around the municipal market. Open till 1800.
Busy and bustling, good for breakfast, snacks and lunch. All serve the same local fare at similar prices.

$ Poc-Chuc
Juárez and Abasolo.
A simple little locals' joint on the corner serving good-value Mexican staples in large portions. Good, cheap and tasty.

Bars and clubs

Fénix Lounge
Playa Norte, next to Na Balam, www.fenixisla.com.
Low-lit and laid-back, Playa Norte's premier beach club and bar often features live music in the evening. In the day time, there's shaded futon beds for chilling out. A fun, casual place and a superb location.

La Adelita
Hidalgo 12.
Adelita stocks over 200 types of tequila, the bar staff really know their stuff and are happy to make recommendations. Pull up a stool, roll up your sleeves – it's going to be a long night.

Rock Bar
Av Hidalgo 8.
As the name suggests, the haunt of spirited rock 'n rollers and other wild things. Great crowd and music at this intimate little downtown bar, not to mention killer cocktails. Cool place, recommended.

The Soggy Peso
Av Rueda Medina, www.soggypeso.com, south out of town, halfway down the airstrip. No under 21s.
This quirky little tiki bar attracts its share of castaways and raconteurs. It's a friendly place, scruffy, unpretentious and laid back. They serve good margaritas and Tex-Mex on the side.

What to do

Diving and snorkelling
There are numerous good dive shops on Isla Mujeres, more than can be mentioned here. 2 established options are:

Carey Dive Center, *Matamoros 13 and Av Rueda Medina, T877-0763, www.careydivecenter.com*. Reef, drift, deep, night and *cenote* dives, PADI certification up to Dive Master, snorkelling and fishing. 2-tank dives cost US$65-140, dependent on destination.

Sea Hawk, offers PADI certification up to Dive Master, deep-sea fishing, snorkelling, and a range of Adventure Dives (2 tanks, US$75-85) including wreck sites, night dives, sleeping shark caves and the MUSA subaquatic museum. They have simple lodging in the attached guesthouse.

Tour operators

Co-operativa Isla Mujeres, *Muelle 7, Av Rueda Medina*. The oldest tourism co-operative on the island, established 1977 and committed to sustainable practice. All their guides are qualified to take tourists to Isla Contoy (US$60 per person). Additionally, they offer sports fishing (US$200, 4 hrs) and snorkelling (US$25).

Co-operativa Isla Bonita, *Av Rueda Medina, T998-897 1095 (Adolfo), find them outside Restaurant Macambo*. This local co-operative specializes in half-day snorkel tours, including dolphin watching, shark handling, and a traditional Yucatec meal (US$25). They also offer trips to Isla Contoy (U$60), fishing (US$200, 4 hrs) and sell *artesanías*.

Transport

Air

The small airstrip in the middle of the island is mainly used for private planes, best arranged with a tourist office in Cancún.

Bicycle, golf cart and moped

Lots of people like to zip around the island in their own transport. You'll find rental places concentrated on the seafront, Av Rueda Medina and the surrounding streets. Rates vary with age and quality of vehicle: bicycles, US$15 per day; mopeds/motorbikes, US$8-11 per hr or US$25-35 per day; golf carts, US$40-50 per day; a credit card is often required as a deposit.

Bus

A public bus runs from the ferry dock to Playa Paraíso every 30 mins, US$0.80. Timings can be erratic, especially on Sun.

Ferry

Ultramar operate ferries to Isla Mujeres every 30 mins from Puerto Juárez, to the north of Cancún (and at slightly higher cost, from the Zona Hotelera); **Magaña Express** ferries depart from their own terminal 2 blocks north of Ultramar.

Taxi

Fixed-rate taxis depart from a rank on Av Rueda Medina, opposite the **HSBC**. A taxi from town to **El Garrafón** and vice versa is US$6. For the return journey, sharing a taxi will work out marginally more expensive than the bus for 4 people. Taxis charge an additional US$1 at night.

Isla Contoy
an uninhabited and strictly protected wildlife refuge

Encompassing 317 ha, Isla Contoy (www.islacontoy.org), 30 km north of Isla Mujeres, is covered in mangroves, tropical forests and white-sand beaches. It is one of the most important seabird nesting sites in the Mexican Caribbean, closely studied by biologists, and home to some 150 migratory and resident avian species, including vociferous colonies of frigates, pelicans and cormorants. Additionally, four species of sea turtle (loggerhead, green, hawksbill and leatherback) nest on the island.

Visitor numbers are limited to 200 per day and only licensed guides may conduct tours (see Isla Mujeres Tour operators, above). Facilities include a visitor centre, museum, souvenir store, observation tower, interpretive trails, resting area with benches and *palapas*. You can snorkel at the Ixlachxé Reef en route to the island.

Isla Holbox
an indolent island with a white-sand beach and colourful village

As yet unspoiled by mass tourism, Isla Holbox, whose name means 'Black Hole' in Yucatec Maya, is a remote and sparsely populated island off the northern coast of Quintana Roo. It has a tiny wood-built village, home to robust fishing people and a small but thriving band of expats. Enclosed by the 154,000-ha Yum Balam Ecological Reserve, Isla Holbox has opportunities for swimming, diving, snorkelling, fishing, kitesurfing and wildlife observation, along with the timeless and strongly recommended pursuit of simply lolling in a hammock.

Sights
Many visitors and locals enjoy a dip in the **Yalahau swimming hole** ⓘ *US$0.80*, a refreshing cold-water spring that has long been an important source of fresh water for islanders; keep an eye out for crocodiles and bring bug repellent.

Offshore, there are several interesting islands and islets, many of them rich in wildlife. **Isla Pájaros** is home to some 140 avian species, mostly waterfowl and seabirds, including pelicans, flamingos, ducks and cormorants. It has two observation towers connected by a walkway designed to minimize human impact. **Isla Pasión**, 15 minutes away by boat, has a white-sand beach with facilities for day trippers. **Cabo Catoche** lies on the mainland 53 km north of Cancún, the point where European explorers are purported to have infamously first set foot on Mexican soil in 1517 (see box, page 40). The area is good for snorkelling and with some planning you can visit the ruins of the ancient church at **Boca Iglesia**, some say the oldest Catholic structure in the country.

From June to September the waters east of Holbox are visited by hundreds of gentle whale sharks, the world's largest fish, who come to feast on plankton blooms and tuna eggs. In the past, the island had a monopoly on tours, but now Cancún is in

ON THE ROAD
First contact: the ill-fated journey of the Santa Lucía

Lost in a small boat in the Caribbean sea, the sight of land must have seemed like divine providence. After 13 days at the mercy of prevailing winds, the band of shipwrecked Spanish travellers were wretched, starved, thirsty and sick. They clambered ashore at Cabo Catoche in Quintana Roo, the first Europeans to set foot in Mexico. But as hordes of hungry Mayan warriors surrounded them, it became clear that their ordeal was only beginning…

The Spaniards had come from the tenuous colony of Santa María la Antigua del Darién, a tempestuous Spanish settlement forged in the wilderness of eastern Panama. In 1511, Captain Enciso y Valdivia had felt compelled to sail to the island of Santo Domingo to report on the colony's troubles – a matter of intrigue had culminated in the exile in a leaky boat of a Spanish nobleman, Diego de Nicuesa, never to be seen again. En route, Valdivia's caravel, the *Santa Lucía*, struck a sandbar and sunk. The 18 survivors were captured by a Mayan chief at Cabo Catoche and, one by one, sacrificed to the gods.

Just two survived. Gerónimo de Aguilar was a devout Franciscan friar from Ecija; Gonzalo Guerrero a sailor from Palos de la Frontera. They escaped but were soon captured and forced into slavery by the Mayan chief Xamanzana.

Months turned to years and Aguilar, who maintained his Catholic vows of celibacy, became a domestic servant for Xamanzana, watching over his wives and daughters. Guerrero ended up in the city of Chaacte'mal (Chetumal), under the dominion of Ah Nachan Kan Xiu, where he impressed the population with his skills in sailing, fishing and carpentry, eventually embraced Mayan customs, and in a historic union of indigenous and Spanish bloodlines, married the chief's daughter, the haughty Zazil Há.

In 1519, Hernán Cortés sailed from Cuba with 500 men, horses and goods for barter and, whilst exploring the island of Cozumel, heard stories about bearded men on the mainland. Following correspondence with messengers, Aguilar soon joined his campaign, becoming a vital informant and translator. But Guerrero remained in the Yucatán, writing to Aguilar: "I am married and have three children, and they look on me as a *cacique* here… My face is tattooed and my ears are pierced. What would the Spaniards say about me if they saw me like this?"

As the Aztec empire fell, Guerrero organized the Maya of the south, teaching them Spanish war craft and strategy. His efforts were not in vain: under the relentless onslaughts of Francisco de Montejo, it took 30 years to subjugate the Yucatán, a bastion of fierce resistance during the conquest of the New World. Guerrero himself died in battle in 1532, having brought 50 war canoes from Chetumal to aid a Honduran *cacique* in his fight against Pedro de Alvarado. Reviled by his 16th-century Spanish compatriots as a traitor, Guerrero is today lauded as a Mexican cultural icon. Misfortune or divine providence, the landing at Cabo Catoche was fateful in so many ways.

on the act, partly because the sharks have begun aggregating closer to Isla Mujeres than Isla Holbox. Despite the good intentions of many ecotourism operators, there are some concerns about lax environmental regulation and unchecked negative impacts. For the moment, whale shark tours cannot be recommended.

Listings Isla Holbox

Tourist information

Most hotels will be able to help with tourist information. Online, consult www.holbox.gob.mx.

Where to stay

$$$ La Palapa
Av Morelos 231, T984-875 2121, www.hotellapalapa.com.
La Palapa is a very comfortable and relaxing boutique lodge on the beach, good for couples and families. They have 19 rooms, studios and bungalows, most with sea view, balconies or wooden verandas. Attentive service, spa therapies available.

$$$ Mawimbi
T984-875 2003, www.mawimbi.com.mx.
An intimate and well-kept boutique hotel with attractive decor and a good reputation. Rooms and bungalows are arty, chic and rustic; very romantic and relaxing. The grounds are private and secluded, yet close to town. Recommended.

$$$-$ Hostel y Cabañas Ida y Vuelta
Av Paseo Kuka, between Robalo y Chacchi, www.holboxhostel.com.
Popular with backpackers and budget travelers, Ida y Vuelta offers accommodation in a private house (**$$$**), simple *cabañas* with sand floors (**$$**), or *cabañas* with a/c and concrete floor (**$$$**). For the ultra-thrifty there are dorm beds, tents or hammocks (**$**).

$$-$ Hostel Tribu
Av Pedro Joaquín Coldwell 19, T984-875 2507, www.tribu hostel.com.
A new hostel, brightly painted, cheerful and brilliantly done. The crowd at **Tribu** is young, fun and sociable. Lots of activities on offer from Spanish lessons to kitesurfing to jam sessions in the bar. Clean, comfortable, simple rooms (**$$**) and dorms (**$**) available. Recommended.

Restaurants

$$$ La Guaya
Calle Palomino s/n, on the plaza. Closed Mon, dinner only.
Creative and authentic Italian cuisine professionally prepared with fresh, organic ingredients. Dishes include seafood, steak cuts and handmade pastas; try the lobster ravioli. Good desserts, cocktails and wine are also available. Gracious service. Recommended.

$$$ Zarabanda
Palomino 249, a block from the plaza.
Long-established Holbox favourite serving typical island cuisine with a Cuban twist. There is an emphasis on fresh seafood and locally sourced ingredients. **Zarabanda** also has a bar and features occasional live music.

$$$-$$ Los Peleones
On the plaza.
An international menu with an emphasis on seafood and Italian. **Los Peleones** offers a laid-back, friendly ambience, quirky *lucha libre* decor, great mojitos and excellent hospitable service. A good spot for watching the coming and going of the town in the plaza below. Recommended.

$$$-$$ Pizzeria Edelyn
On the plaza.
There are certainly better Italian restaurants in town, but **Edelyn** is casual, reliable and local, and open late. Most people rate their famous thin-crust lobster pizza quite highly, but don't expect gourmet. A good place to see local life.

$$-$ La Tortillería
Tiburón Ballena. Open breakfast and lunch only.
A modest and friendly little eatery run by a young Spanish couple. They serve great Spanish tortillas, good salads, smoothies, coffee, pies and vegetarian dishes. Recommended.

Cafés and bakeries

Le Jardin
Calle Lisa.
An authentic French bakery and café serving croissants, baguettes, sandwiches, fruit and omelettes. Good coffee and muffins too.

Transport

Isla Holbox
Bicycle and golf cart hire
There are no cars on the island, but golf carts and bicycle rentals are available.

Ferry
Ferries to Isla Holbox depart from the town of **Chiquilá**, hourly, 0600-2130, US$6.25. Public transport to Chiquilá is infrequent, 4 buses daily from **Cancún**, 3½ hrs, US$8. If driving, there are car parks in Chiquilá, US$2-3 daily.

South on the Riviera Maya
sandy beach resorts strung along the Caribbean coast

Formerly known as the 'Cancún–Tulum Corridor', the Mayan Riviera unfolds along the Caribbean shore with a procession of luminous white-sand bays, fishing villages, lively beach towns, gated resort complexes, palatial health spas and immaculately manicured lawns, where the only sounds to disturb your meditations are the occasional thwack of a club and the persistent hiss of water sprinklers. There isn't much authentically Mayan about it, but a lot of businesses trade shamelessly on the beauty and exoticism of Mayan culture.

Adventure parks
The exact boundaries of the Riviera, a marketing concept introduced in 1999, appear to be expanding too. Once limited to a stretch of the Federal Highway, some maps now show it engulfing half the state of Quintana Roo from Isla Holbox to Felipe Carrillo Puerto. Whatever its limits, the service and convenience of the Riviera between Cancún and Tulum will appeal to families, especially its

ecologically themed adventure parks, which make fun use of caves, *cenotes*, lagoons and beaches.

Near Playa del Carmen, perhaps the oldest and most famous is **Xcaret** ⓘ *www.xcaret.com.mx, US$89*, built on the ruins of a Mayan port. Its theatrical displays are iffy, but many visitors enjoy the outdoor element. **Xplor** ⓘ *www.xplor.travel, US$109 adults, US$55 children*, is a new one, offering zip-lining, amphibious vehicles and other adrenaline-charged thrills. Further south, 13 km from Tulum, **Xel-Ha** ⓘ *www.xelha.com, US$79 adults, US40 children*, is an aquatic park with snorkelling, tubing through mangroves and other water-based activities. You can get a package for all three parks: US$197 adults, US$149 children; note certain experiences may cost extra. And there are more: **Labna Ha Ecopark Adventures** ⓘ *Cancún–Tulum Km 240, T984-100 1362, www.labnaha.com*; and near the resort of Akumal, **Parque Natural Aktun Chen** ⓘ *T984-806 4962, www.aktunchen.com*; both these offer a cave, *cenote* and zip-line combo.

Puerto Morelos

Despite the advent of tourism and a more than tenfold population increase in the last 10 years, Puerto Morelos, 34 km south of Cancún, has managed to retain the intimacy of its former existence as a fishing village, for now. Look out for the tilted lighthouse, an emblem of the port that has survived some of the region's worst hurricanes since 1967.

Many travellers find relief in Puerto's lazy ambience: the dusty main plaza overlooks the beach, a handful of roads skirt the mangroves. For divers and snorkellers, the **Mesoamerican Barrier Reef**, the second largest reef system in the world, lies just 500 m offshore. To get to Puerto Morelos, public transport from Cancún drops passengers on the Carretera Cancún–Chetumal, every 15 minutes; it's 2 km to the beach on an access road; bus US$0.70, taxi US$3; you can walk but cover up and bring insect repellent. Back on the highway, there's an interesting botanical garden by Dr Alfredo Barrera Marín, **Yaax Che** ⓘ *Carretera Cancún–Chetmual Km 320, T998-206 9233, www.ecosur.mx/jb/YaaxChe, Mon-Sat 0900-1700*, and a zoo.

Playa del Carmen → *See map, page 44.*

Unlike Cancún, the entertainment hub of Playa del Carmen has not evolved into a gritty metropolitan sprawl, but it doesn't glisten either; few of its buildings exceed four storeys and most of the action is concentrated into a relatively small downtown area. And yet 'Playa', as it is affectionately known, is to the European tourist what Cancún is to the North American: a well-oiled resort where you are invited to gorge your appetites, flop about on the sand and forget about the world of toil you left behind. Fun, perhaps, but something got lost in the throng of gaudy souvenir stores, fast-food joints, jewellers, boutiques and department stores and, just like Cancún, you'll either love it or hate it.

Many travellers use Playa as a base for exploring ruins and *cenotes* in the region, otherwise there isn't much to do besides the obvious: eat, shop and drink. The town is laid out on a grid with most establishments within walking distance. Day and night, the herds ramble up and down the main commercial drag, **Quinta Avenida** (Fifth Avenue), a pedestrianized thoroughfare running from Calle 1 Norte to Calle 40. During high season, the swell of crowds and persistent attention of touts can be tiresome (just keep smiling). The **beach**, two blocks east of Quinta Avenida, is lovely and somewhat redeeming. The main plaza, next to the ADO bus terminal, has an intimate, modern church. In the afternoon, you'll see Totonac dancers – *voladores* – from Veracruz State, who spiral down a 30-m-high pole with rope around their ankles; please tip kindly if you watch the show.

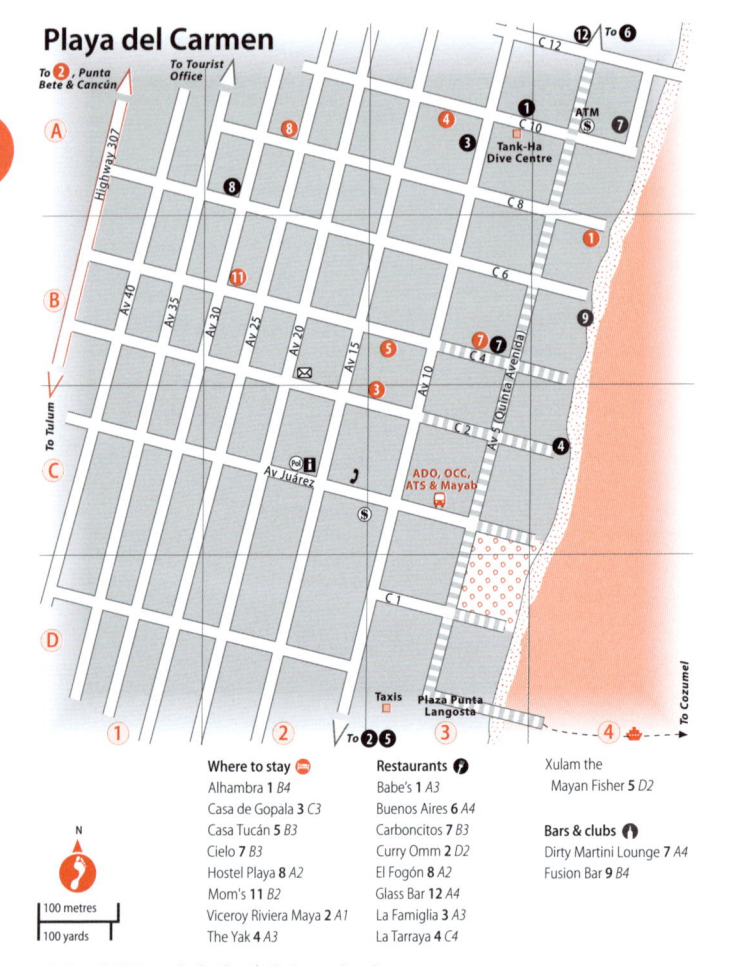

Playa del Carmen

Where to stay
Alhambra **1** *B4*
Casa de Gopala **3** *C3*
Casa Tucán **5** *B3*
Cielo **7** *B3*
Hostel Playa **8** *A2*
Mom's **11** *B2*
Viceroy Riviera Maya **2** *A1*
The Yak **4** *A3*

Restaurants
Babe's **1** *A3*
Buenos Aires **6** *A4*
Carboncitos **7** *B3*
Curry Omm **2** *D2*
El Fogón **8** *A2*
Glass Bar **12** *A4*
La Famiglia **3** *A3*
La Tarraya **4** *C4*
Xulam the Mayan Fisher **5** *D2*

Bars & clubs
Dirty Martini Lounge **7** *A4*
Fusion Bar **9** *B4*

44•Cancún & Yucatán Peninsula Quintana Roo State

Listings South on the Riviera Maya *map p44*

Where to stay

Puerto Morelos

$$$ Rancho Sak-Ol Libertad
Next door to Caribbean Reef Club, T998-871 0181, www.ranchosakol.com.
Pleasant B&B accommodation in 2-storey thatched bungalows; each unit has a wooden terrace and hammock for chilling out. A very tranquil, restful spot, right next to the beach. Spa therapies, shared kitchen and snorkelling gear available. Recommended.

$$ Posada Amor
Av Javier Rojo Gómez, opposite the beach, T998-871 0033, www.posada-amor.wix.com/puertom.
A small, charming *posada*, well established and affordable, but also quite simple with no frills. A good central location, fine restaurant-bar and friendly Mexican owners.

Playa del Carmen

Accommodation in Playa del Carmen is generally expensive and poor value compared to other parts of Mexico, particularly around the beach and Av 5. The prices given below are for the high season and can drop by as much as 50% at other times of the year.

$$$$ Viceroy Riviera Maya
Playa Xcalacoco, Fracc 7, 10 km north of Playa del Carmen, T984-877 3000, www.viceroyhotelsandresorts.com.
Secluded, exclusive, chic and tasteful, this impeccable spa resort on the beach has 41 luxurious villas in a verdant jungle setting, and excellent, attentive service. A host of facilities include pool, sun deck and gym.

$$$$-$$$ Alhambra
Calle 8 Norte con playa, T984-873 0735, www.alhambra-hotel.net.
The interior of the family-run **Alhambra** has a light, clean, airy, palatial feel. All rooms have balcony or sea view and general amenities include yoga instruction, jacuzzi, massage, spa and excellent restaurant. Quiet and peaceful, despite its setting near beach bars. French and English spoken. Recommended.

$$$ Casa de Gopala
Calle 2 Norte s/n, entre Av 10 y 15 Centro, T984-873 0054, www.casadegopala.com.
The interior of **Casa de Gopala** is handsomely attired in traditional Mexican style. The rooms are spacious, airy and comfortable, but the suite has more character. There's a dive shop, rooftop pool, relaxing garden and jacuzzi. Helpful staff.

$$$ Hotel Cielo
Calle 4, between 5 and 10, T984-873 1227, www.hotelcielo.com.
Appropriately named **Hotel Cielo** boasts commanding views from its rooftop terrace. Located just off Av 5, accommodation includes standard rooms, *cabañas* and studios, all tastefully attired in traditional Mexican style. Rates include a 50% breakfast discount in **Carboncitos** restaurant, 10% off other meals. Good service, cheaper if paying cash.

$$$-$$ Casa Tucán
Calle 4 Norte, between Av 10 and 15, T984-873 0283, www.casa tucan.de.
German-owned hotel with simple, rustic *cabañas*, studios and no-frills

rooms. The grounds are rambling and labyrinthine with a lovely lush garden, painted murals and a deep pool where diving instruction takes place.

$$$-$$ Mom's Hotel
Calle 4 and Av 30, about 5 blocks from bus station or beach, T984-873 0315, www.momshotel.com.
Excellent value, friendly, family-run hotel with pleasant, colourful rooms and a small pool. There are also studios and apartments and good rates for long-term stays. The attached restaurant serves international food in the evening. Recommended.

$$-$ Hostel Playa
Av 25 with Calle 8, T984-803 3277, www.hostelplaya.com.
There's a comfortable, friendly atmosphere at this well-maintained and professionally run hostel. Amenities include a single- and mixed-sex dorms ($), private rooms ($$), a superb, well-equipped shared kitchen, lounge space, paddling pool and rooftop *palapa*. Shared bathrooms are clean. Recommended for backpackers and solo budget travellers.

$$-$ The Yak
Calle 10 Norte, between Av 10 and 15, T984-148 0925, www.yakhostel.com.
A bohemian new hostel, very intimate and friendly, and home to a sociable backpacker scene. They offer clean, homely rooms ($$), dorm beds ($), shared kitchen, popular bar and garden, and activities such as movie night. Good hosts, good reports.

Restaurants

Puerto Morelos

$$$ El Merkadito
Rafael Melgar lote 8-B, www.elmerkadito.mx.
Perched on the edge of the beach, **El Merkadito** is a popular seafood restaurant that serves hearty plates of octopus *tostadas*, shrimp ceviche, tuna steak, marlin tacos and more. A casual option with open-air seating under a terraced palm-thatched *palapa*.

$$-$ El Nicho
Av Tulum and Rojo Gómez, www.elnicho.com.mx. Closes 1400.
Laid-back, pleasant, low-key eatery serving great brunch and breakfasts, including most excellent eggs benedict. Good juices, waffles, coffee and iced tea. Mexican staples served at lunchtime.

Playa del Carmen
The majority of the town's restaurants line Quinta Avenida, where most tourists limit themselves and a meal costs no less (and usually a bit more) than US$10. Popular, big-name restaurants dominate the southern end of the street. Quieter, subtler settings lie north, beyond Calle 20. For budget eating, head west, away from the main drag.

$$$ Buenos Aires
5a Av and Calle 34.
Probably the best meat dishes in town, professionally prepared and authentically Argentine. Offerings include succulent cuts of fillet and mixed grill platters. Occasional displays of tango dancing.

$$$ Curry Omm
10a Av and Calle 3 Sur, www.letseat.at/Curryomm.

Great, authentic Indian cuisine, good and spicy. Offerings include old favourites like samosas, papadums and naan, a range of hearty curries, including masala, madras and vindaloo, along with tasty traditional drinks such as mango lassi and chai. Great friendly service. Recommended.

$$$ The Glass Bar
5a Av and Calle 12, www.theglassbar.com.mx.
The place for an intimate, romantic dinner, **The Glass Bar** is a sophisticated Italian restaurant serving Mediterranean cuisine and seafood. It is recommended chiefly for its stock of fine wine, however, a rarity in Playa.

$$$ Xulam the Mayan Fisher
10a Av and Calle 3 Sur, www.xulam.com.mx.
Good seafood and traditional Mayan dishes, creatively prepared and presented. The themed decor is reminiscent of a ruined Mayan temple, complete with archaeological relics, colourful chattering parrots and creeping vegetation. Touristy, but lots of fun.

$$$-$$ Babe's
Calle 10, between 5a and 10a Av, www.babesnoodlesandbar.com.
Casual Thai noodle bar with kitsch decor and a superb menu of red, yellow and green curries, spring rolls, samosas, soups and more. Belting flavours, decent service and a fine stock of liquor at the bar. Highly recommended.

$$$-$$ Carboncitos
Calle 4, between 5a and 10a Av.
Seafood and steaks with a Mexican twist. Popular offerings include grilled jumbo shrimps, the salsa sampler and the frozen mojitos. Breakfast is very good too, try the *huevos rancheros*. Good service with al fresco dining on the pedestrian street. Recommended.

$$ La Famiglia
10a Av and Calle 10.
In a town with no shortage of Italian restaurants, **La Famiglia** is one of the better and more affordable ones. They serve wholesome traditional fare from the motherland, including handmade pastas, lasagne and stone-baked pizzas. Casual dining.

$$-$ El Fogón
Av 30 and Calle 6.
A buzzing locals' joint, hugely popular and economical. They serve grilled meat, wholesome *tortas*, tacos, quesadillas and other Mexican staples. Highly recommended.

$$-$ La Tarraya
Calle 2 and the beach.
Economical seafood on the shore, including shrimp tacos and fried whole fish. Very simple and no frills, sometimes hit and miss, but a nice place to soak up ocean views and knock back a beer or two. Check your bill.

Bars and clubs

Playa del Carmen
Playa competes with Cancún as a major entertainment hub. Overall, the scene is a little quieter and more nuanced, offering many down-to-earth alternatives alongside the usual big-name clubs like **Coco Bongo** and **Señor Frog**.

Dirty Martini Lounge
1a Av, between Calle 10 and 12.
There's a good boozy atmosphere at the **Dirty Martini Lounge**, the place to settle in for a long, hard drink. Fun crowd,

seasoned bartenders and no shortage of Martini, naturally.

Fusion Bar
Calle 6 and the beach, www.fusionhotelmexico.com.
One of the better beach lounges, **Fusion Bar** has a romantic ambience with low-lighting rustic oil lanterns, tables and *palapas* on the sand. They often feature live music in the evenings and the kitchen serves good food.

What to do

Playa del Carmen

Diving and snorkelling
The Abyss, *T984-876 3285, www.abyssdivecenter.com.* **The Abyss** is a professional, first-rate operation with more than 14 years' experience of local waters. Owned and managed by Canadian Dave Tomlinson, who offers ocean and *cenote* dives, certification, and a host of specialized and technical training. No physical premises, contact in advance by email.
Tank-Ha, *T984-873 0302, www.tankha.com.* The only dive shop in town with a licence to go to Cozumel, cutting out the ferry trip. They offer certification up to Dive Master, speciality courses, ocean and *cenote* dives, as well as the interesting option to hunt lion fish, an invasive species that apparently makes good ceviche.

Tour operators
Alltournative, *Carretera Chetumal–Puerto Juárez Km 287, T984-803 9999, www.alltournative.com.* A well-established ecotourism 'pioneer' with a proven commitment to sustainability. They offer adventure tours to the Yucatán's *cenotes* and national parks, as well as cultural visits to archaeological sites and Mayan communities.

Transport

Puerto Morelos
Bus
ADO buses (and others) travelling between Cancún and Playa del Carmen stop on the Carretera Cancún–Chetumal outside Puerto Morelos every 15 mins. Taxi to/from the beach, US$3.

Playa del Carmen
Bus
The **ADO** bus terminal is on the corner of Av Juárez and Quinta Avenida (5a Av).
To **Cancún**, frequent departures, 1½ hrs, US$4; 2nd-class services with **Mayab**, less frequent, US$3. To **Cancún airport**, frequent between 0700 and 1915, 1 hr, US$10. To **Chetumal**, ADO, frequent departures, 4½ hrs, US$21; and many 2nd-class buses. To **Chichén Itzá**, ADO, 0800, 4 hrs, US$22; also with 2nd-class buses bound for Mérida. To **Cobá**, ADO, 0800, 0900, 1000, 2 hrs, US$7. To **Mérida**, frequent departures, 5 hrs, US$28. To **San Cristóbal de las Casas**, OCC, 1715, 2155, 16 hrs, US$66; an ADO

Language schools

Playalingua, *Calle 20 between Av 5 and 10, T984-873 3876, www.playalingua.com.* Weekend excursions, a/c, library, family stays, from US$225 per week (20 hrs).
Solexico Language and Cultural Center, *Av 35 between 6 and 6 bis, T984-873 0755, www.solexico.com.* Variable programme with workshops, also have schools in Oaxaca and Puerto Vallarta.

GL, 1900, US$78. To **Tulum**, frequent departures, 1 hr, US$6; many 2nd class. To **Valladolid**, frequent, 3 hrs, US$12.50 (most buses going to Mérida stop at Valladolid. 2nd-class buses to Valladolid go via Tulum). To **Xcaret**, frequent departures, 15 mins, US$4. To **Xel Há**, frequent departures, 1 hr, US$5.

Car
Car hire Alamo, 5a Av and Calle 6 Norte, T984-826 6893, www.alamo.com; **Fiesta**, Av 144 No 35, T984-803 3345, www.fiestacarrental.com; **Hertz**, 5a Av between Calles 10 and 12, T984-873 0703, www.hertz.com; and many others.

Ferry
Ferries to **Cozumel** depart from the main dock, just off the plaza. There are 2 competing companies, **Ultramar**, T998 843-2011, www.granpuerto.com.mx, and right next door, **Mexico Water Jets**, T987-879 3112, www.mexicowaterjets.com.mx, departures every 2-4 hrs each from 0500 until 2200, US$11.50 one way. Buy ticket 1 hr before journey. Car ferries to Cozumel, 4 daily (2 on Sun) with **Transcaribe**, www.transcaribe.net, family-sized car US$60, departing from Calica (Punta Venado) south of Playa del Carmen, but they will not transport rental vehicles.

Taxi
Cancún airport US$40 for 4 persons. Tours to **Tulum** and **Xel-Há** from kiosk by boat dock US$35-40; tours to Tulum, Xel-Há and **Xcaret**, 5-6 hrs, US$60-70; taxi to Xcaret US$10. Taxis congregate on the Av Juárez side of the square (**Sindicato Lázaro Cárdenas del Río**, T998-873 0032).

Cozumel

a mecca for divers

The 'discovery' and popularization of Isla Cozumel and its dazzling coral reefs is often incorrectly attributed to the French oceanographer and documentary filmmaker, Jacques Cousteau. In fact, it was a Mexican director, René Cardona, who first documented Cozumel's vivid underwater world with his 1957 film *Un Mundo Nuevo* (he was, to an extent, inspired by Cousteau's 1956 explorations of the Mediterranean and Red Sea in *Un Monde du Silence*). Cousteau himself did visit the island in 1960 and famously declared, "Cozumel is one of the best places around the world for diving, thanks to its fantastic visibility and its wonderful marine life…" but by then, the word was already out.

Today, despite more than 50 years of touristic development, the controversial intrusion of cruise ships and the devastating impact of hurricanes, many of Cozumel's reefs remain healthy and vibrant, if endangered. Isla Cozumel, the largest of Mexico's Caribbean islands, continues to serve as a world-class dive destination.

Sights
The town, **San Miguel de Cozumel**, is touristic and commercial, increasingly marketed to cruise ship passengers arriving from Miami and Cancún, and lacking much nightlife or a discernible personality, a rather uninspired and

overpriced destination. There isn't much to detain you apart from the **Museo de la Isla** ⓘ *Calle 4 and 6, Mon-Sat 0900-1600, US$2.50*, which charts the historical development of Cozumel.

Similarly, the island's beaches are pleasant enough, but not worth a special trip from the mainland. The northern and western shores are generally sandy and good for swimming (poor for snorkelling), if a bit narrow; popular stretches include **Playa San Francisco** ⓘ *US$8*, with a beach club that caters to cruisers and, 14 km south of town, **Playa Paradise**, also resort-style. Swimming on the rugged, exposed east coast is very dangerous due to ocean underflows; the exception is the sheltered bay at **Chen Río**. Surfers could try **Punta Morena**.

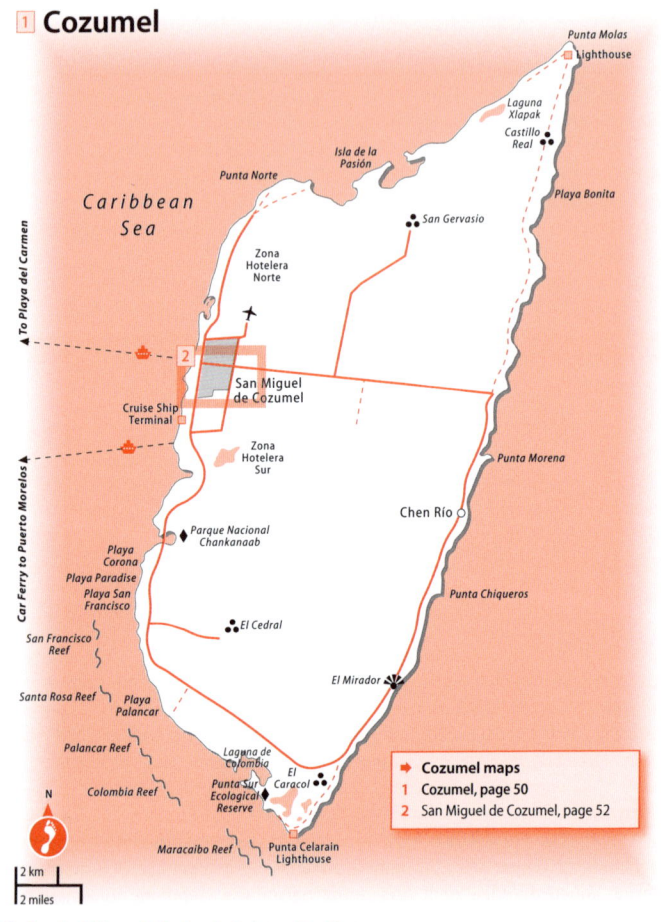

Cozumel

➤ Cozumel maps
1 Cozumel, page 50
2 San Miguel de Cozumel, page 52

Like the Mayan Riviera, Cozumel now boasts adventure parks for day-trippers. Perched between a lagoon and a sandy beach, **Parque Chankanaab** ⓘ *Carretera Costera Sur Km 9.5, www.cozumelparks.com, Mon-Sat 0800-1600, US$21, children US$14, some activities cost extra*, offers a world of fun including botanical garden, crocodile sanctuary, spa facilities, dolphinarium, snorkelling, restaurants, hammocks and *palapas*. **Punta Sur Park** ⓘ *Carretera Costera Sur Km 30, T987-872 0914, www.cozumelparks.com, Mon-Sat 0900-1600, US$12, children US$8, some activities cost extra*, is a much wilder 1-sq-km ecological park encompassing reefs, beaches and lagoons. Sights include the **Celarain lighthouse**, now converted to a nautical museum, Mayan ruins (see below) and wildlife observation towers.

★ Dive sites

Cozumel's reef system is part of the Mesoamerican Barrier Reef with sections on the southern side of the island protected by the 120 sq km **Parque Nacional Arrecifes de Cozumel**. There are dozens of sites to suit beginners and advanced divers. Favourites include **Palancar Reef**, which has deep and shallow sections, impressive coral outcrops, troughs and canyons. **Santa Rosa Wall** is a steep vertical shelf with very impressive blooms. **Colombia Reef** has shallow sections with a pretty coral garden and gentle currents; the deep section has massive corals and swim-throughs where you are likely to glimpse pelagic species. For more experienced divers, the reefs at **Punta Sur**, **Maracaibo** and **Baracuda** should not to be missed. Almost all Cozumel diving is drift diving, so if you are not used to a current, choose an operator you feel comfortable with. Snorkelling on Isla Cozumel is possible, but many sites were badly damaged by Hurricane Wilma in 2005 and have not yet recovered.

Archaeological sites

Inhabited from 300 AD, Cozumel, whose name means 'Island of Swallows' in Yucatec Maya, was an ancient centre of worship for Ixchel. The journey to her temples involved a perilous passage by sea canoe and her pilgrims, according to the Bishop of Yucatán in the 16th century, Diego de Landa, "held Cozumel in the same veneration as we have for pilgrimages to Jerusalem and Rome". Sadly, the mysteries of Cozumel were lost forever after the Spaniards brought a devastating plague of small pox.

Today, all that remains are some 32 very modest archaeological sites, mostly single buildings thought to have been lookouts and navigational aids. The most interesting and easy to reach (and therefore often overrun with tour groups) is the post-Classic site of **San Gervasio** ⓘ *Carretera Transversal Km 7, 0800-1545, US$8, Spanish-speaking guides are on hand, US$18*. There are *sacbés* (sacred roads) between the groups of buildings, no large or monumental structures, but an interesting plaza and an arch, and surviving pigment in places. The site is located in the north of the island, 7 km from San Miguel, then 6 km to the left up a paved road, toll US$1; taxis are expensive, US$45 with two-hour wait; consider cycling. **Castillo Real** is one of many sites on the northeastern coast, but the road to this part of the island is in bad condition and the ruins themselves are very small. **El Cedral** in the southwest (3 km from the main island road) is a two-room temple, overgrown with trees, in the centre of the village of the same name. **El Caracol**, where the sun in the form of a shell was worshipped, is 1 km from the southernmost Punta Celarain.

Listings Cozumel *maps p50 and p52*

Tourist information

Tourist office
Plaza del Sol, Av 5 Sur, between Av Juárez and Calle 1 Sur, upstairs above the bank, T987-869 0211, www.cozumel.travel. Mon-Fri 0800-1500.
Maps, flyers and general information.

Where to stay

$$$ Flamingo
Calle 6 Norte 81, T987-872 1264, www.hotelflamingo.com.
An intimate boutique lodging with a range of rooms and a penthouse suite, all spacious, tastefully attired and

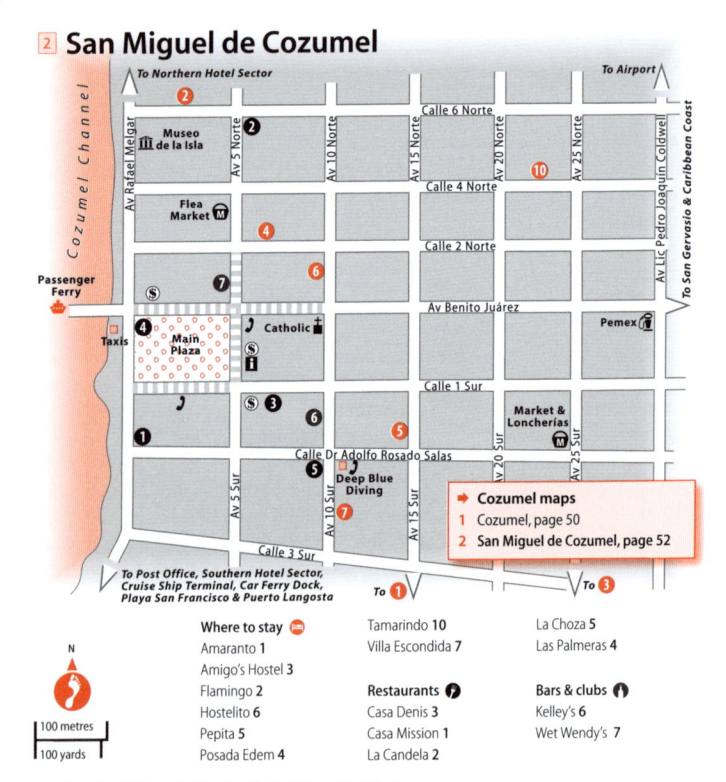

San Miguel de Cozumel

➡ **Cozumel maps**
1 Cozumel, page 50
2 San Miguel de Cozumel, page 52

Where to stay
Amaranto **1**
Amigo's Hostel **3**
Flamingo **2**
Hostelito **6**
Pepita **5**
Posada Edem **4**
Tamarindo **10**
Villa Escondida **7**

La Choza **5**
Las Palmeras **4**

Restaurants
Casa Denis **3**
Casa Mission **1**
La Candela **2**

Bars & clubs
Kelley's **6**
Wet Wendy's **7**

equipped with modern conveniences. Spa, diving and sports fishing packages available, see website for more. Friendly and helpful staff.

$$$ Tamarindo
Calle 4 Norte 421, between Av 20 and 25, T987-872 6190, www.tamarindobedandbreakfast.com.
This tranquil B&B accommodation is located in a residential street and offers restful rooms and a leafy garden complete with plunge pool. A second property near the seafront has apartments and bungalows.

$$$ Villa Escondida
Av 10 Sur 299, T987-120 1225, www.villaescondidacozumel.com.
Villa Escondida is a cosy B&B with 4 very clean, comfortable rooms and a well-tended garden with hammocks and plunge pool. Breakfasts are excellent and the Canadian/Mexican owners, David and Magda, are great hosts. Adults only. Recommended.

$$ Amaranto
Calle 5 Sur, between Av 15 and 20, T987-872-3219, www.amarantobedandbreakfast.com.
Attractive thatched-roof Mayan-style bungalows and suites, complete with hammocks and kitchenettes. Spanish, English and French are spoken by the owners, Elaine and Jorge. There's a pool, and childcare is available on request. Rustic, tasteful and good value. Recommended.

$$ Pepita
Av 15 Sur 120 y Calle 1 Sur, T987-872 0098, www.hotelpepitacozumel.com.
A well-established and family-run budget hotel with simple rooms set around a plant-filled courtyard, each with fridge and a/c. Clean, quiet and inexpensive for the island. Free coffee in the morning.

$$-$ Amigos Hostel
Calle 7 Sur 571, between Av 30 and 25, T987-872 3868, www.cozumelhostel.com.
Formerly a B&B, **Amigos Hostels** features a large leafy garden with pool, various communal areas, a shady *palapa*, pool table, hammocks, simple shared kitchen, mixed dorms ($) and clean rooms ($$). The owner, Kathy, has lots of information about the island.

$$-$ Hostelito
Av 10 No 42, between Juárez and 2 Nte, T987-869 8157, www.hostelito.com.mx.
This downtown backpackers' hostel has large dorms ($) and simple whitewashed rooms ($$), suites, sun-decks and a shared kitchen. Clean and hip.

$ Posada Edém
Calle 2 Norte 124, T987-872 1166, gustarimo@hotmail.com.
Very basic, economical rooms with Wi-Fi and the usual bare necessities, including fan or a/c. A little run down these days, but friendly.

Restaurants

There are few eating options for budget travellers. The cheapest places for breakfast, lunch or an early dinner are the *loncherías* next to the market on A R Salas, between Av 20 and 25. They serve fairly good local *comida corrida*, 0800-1930.

$$$ Casa Mission
Av 55, between Juárez and Calle 1 Sur, www.missioncoz.com. Daily 1700-2300.
Established in 1973, this restaurant survived hurricanes Wilma and Gilbert and is now a Cozumel institution. Fine Mexican, international and seafood

in an elegant hacienda setting. Recommended.

$$$ La Choza
Salas 198 and Av 10, www.lachozarestaurant.com.
A large, airy restaurant serving classic Mexican dishes, seafood and regional cuisine. Good service and atmosphere, colourful decor. Popular with both tourists and nationals.

$$ La Candela
Calle 5 Norte 298. Closed Sun.
Modest and affordable little restaurant serving good breakfasts and set lunches, Cuban and Mexican staples, including fish tacos. A Cozumel favourite with pleasant service.

$$ Las Palmeras
At the pier, Av Melgar, www.restaurantepalmeras.com. Open 0700-1400.
Las Palmeras serves reliable and wholesome grub, a popular spot for breakfast. The restaurant overlooks the pier and is a great place for people-watching.

$$-$ Casa Denis
Calle 1 Sur 164, close to plaza, www.casadenis.com.
A charming, intimate little eatery, one of the oldest on the island, owned by Denis and Juanita Angulo. They serve excellent and affordable tacos, tortas and other Mexican fare. Former diners include Jackie Onassis. Recommended.

Bars and clubs

The big-name clubs like Señor Frog's and Carlos 'n' Charlie are clustered around the pier. They tend to draw tourists and very few locals. For something casual, try:

Kelley's
Av 10, www.kelleyscozumel.com.
A grungy Irish sports bar, recommended chiefly because it serves beer on tap, including Guinness. Bring pesos, poor exchange rate.

Wet Wendy's
Av 5, between Calle 2 and Juárez, www.wetwendys.com.
A popular place serving the most insane margaritas anywhere. Wet Wendy, the bar's namesake, is a legendary local mermaid, not an adult entertainer.

What to do

Diving
There are 2 different types of dive centre: the larger ones, where the divers are taken out to sea in big boats with many passengers; the smaller, more personalized dive shops, with a maximum of 8 people per small boat, some of which are recommended below:

Deep Blue, *A R Salas 200, corner of Av 10 Sur, T987-872 5653, www.deepbluecozumel.com.* A PADI facility since 1995, **Deep Blue** specializes in deep dives, including trips to Punta Sur, Maracaibo and Barracuda reefs. They also offer PADI, NAUI and SSI certification up to Dive Master. All dives are computerized for maximum bottom time and increased safety. Helpful and knowledgeable.

Scuba Tony, *Av Xel Ha 151, T987-869 8268, www.scubatony.com.* Tony loves diving so much he quit an 11-year career with the Los Angeles Sheriff's department to establish a dive shop on Cozumel. He offers reef, twilight and night dives, certification up to Advanced Open Water, private charters and accommodation. No physical premises, contact through the website.

Transport

Air
The airport is just north of the town with a minibus shuttle service to the hotels.

There are 10-min flights to and from the airstrip near Playa del Carmen, as well as flights linking to **Mexico City**, **Cancún** and some international destinations.

Bicycle and moped
The best way to get around the island is by hired moped or bicycle. Mopeds cost US$25-35 per day, credit card needed as deposit; bicycles are around US$15-20 per day, US$20 cash or TC deposit. Rental stalls at the ferry terminal, or try **El Aguila**, Av Melgar, between 3 and 5 Sur, T987-872 0729; and **El Dorado**, Av Juárez, between 5 and 10, T987-872 2383.

Bus
There are no buses, but Cozumel town is small enough to visit on foot, or you can hire a moped or bicycle (see above) or take a taxi (see below).

Car
Car rental There are many agencies, including **Avis**, airport, T987-872 0219; **Budget**, Av 5 between 2 and 4 Norte, T987-872 0219; **Hertz**, Av Melgar, T987-872 3955.

Ferry
The passenger ferry to and from Playa del Carmen runs every 2 hrs and the car ferry leaves 4 times daily from **Calica**, south of Playa del Carmen (see page 49).

Taxi
Taxis are plentiful. Beware taxis looking for kick-backs.

Tulum

clifftop compact Mayan site overlooking the turquoise Caribbean

Perched high on a sea cliff overlooking the eastern horizon, Tulum was originally named Zama, meaning 'City of the Dawn' in Yucatec Maya. Rising to prominence during the late post-Classic era (1200-1450 AD), it was an important trade hub where itinerant merchants exchanged precious commodities such as obsidian, jade and copper. Home to approximately 1500 inhabitants, the settlement was accessed by sea canoe through a gap in the offshore reef. The word 'Tulum' means wall or fence in Maya and the entire city was surrounded by walls, partially standing today.

Tulum ruins

www.inah.gob.mx, 0800-1700, US$4.50, parking, US$2.50, guides US$20. Buses drop passengers 1 km from the ruins at an access road on the Carretera Cancún–Chetumal. Taxis from Tulum village, US$5.50. The site is very popular and swamped with tour groups after 0900 or 1000.

Compared with the jungle-shrouded metropolizes further inland, Tulum is a very small site, easily explored in an hour or two. Its buildings are small, squat versions of the architecture at Chichén Itzá, very typical of the east coast style. The **Temple of the Descending God** contains a well-preserved stucco sculpture of a downward diving deity, a recurring motif and the personification of the setting sun, to whom all west-facing buildings were consecrated. Nearby, the **Temple of Frescoes** was an observatory for tracking the sun. The façades of its inner temple have murals depicting deities and serpents, sadly no longer open to the public; its outer temple has stucco figures in bas-relief, including masks on the corners. The grandest building in Tulum is **El Castillo**, a fortress-like structure built in several phases on the edge of the cliff. It contains shrines and vaulted rooms, but you are not permitted to climb its steps. Bring a swimsuit if you want to scramble down from the ruins to one of the beaches for a swim. Do not attempt to swim out to the reef, 600 m to 1 km away.

Tulum town

Approximately 3 km from the ruins, Tulum town, until recently, was nothing more than a dusty strip of houses on the edge of the highway. Today it is blossoming into a minor tourist town complete with international restaurants, coffee houses, dive shops and lodgings to suit all budgets. You'll find the ADO bus terminal and taxi ranks on the Carretera Cancún–Chetumal, which changes its name to Avenida Tulum as it enters the town. A small tourist information kiosk, irregularly staffed, is on the plaza. Just outside town, on the highway to Cobá, you'll find the **Tulum Monkey Sanctuary** ⓘ *T984-115 4296, www.tulummonkeysanctuary.com*, a private reserve with many spider monkeys and two refreshing *cenotes*; reservations essential.

Tulum beach

Fronted by a procession of luxury hotels, upscale boutiques, B&Bs and *cabañas*, the sublime white-sand beach running south of the ruins was 'discovered' by property speculators some years ago. The treatment has been relatively rustic and low-rise (many establishments lack electricity during daylight hours), but there are now limited economical lodging options on this fabled stretch. If determined, you may find a scruffy cabin with a sand floor and shared bathroom for around US$30, but you should bring padlocks, carefully check the security situation and consider stashing valuables elsewhere. Access to the beach is via the Carretera Tulum–Boca

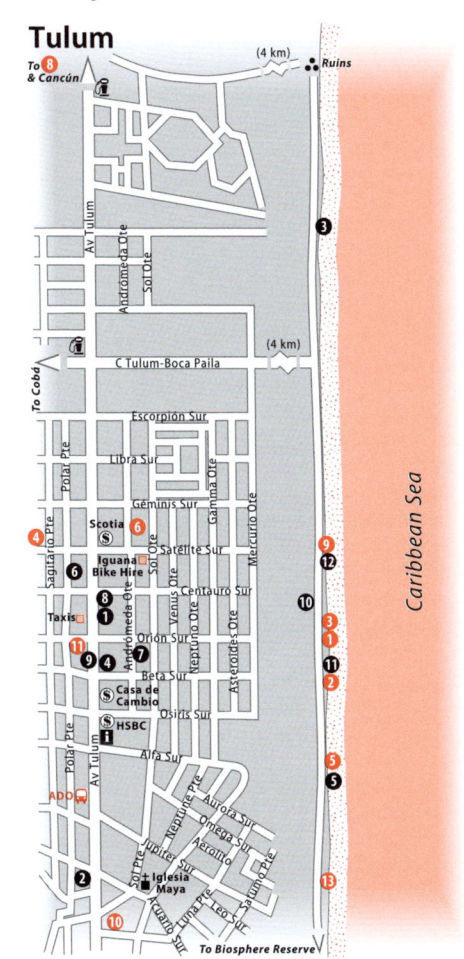

Tulum

Where to stay
Ahau Tulum 2
Cabañas La Luna 3
Dos Ceibas 13
Hostel Sheck 4
Los Arrecifes 1
Nueva Vida de Ramiro 5
Posada 6 6
Posada Los Mapaches 8
Posada Luna del Sur 10
Posada Margherita 9
Suites Nadet 11

Restaurants
Doña Tinas 2
El Gourmet 1
El Pequeño Buenos Aires 4
Ginger 6
La Gloria de Don Pepe 7
La Malquerida 8
La Nave 9
La Zebra 5
Margherita 12
Mezzanine 3
Restaurare 10
Ziggy's 11

Paila, which branches south from a crossroad on the Carretera Cancún–Chetumal and skirts the shore as far as Punta Allen. Taxis from the town to the beach US$5.50 minimum; cycling is an option.

Around Tulum

ruined Mayan city, jungle-fringed lake and vast biosphere

Cobá
www.inah.gob.mx, 0800-1700, US$4.50.

An important Mayan city in the eighth and ninth centuries AD, whose population is estimated to have been between 40,000 and 50,000, Cobá was abandoned for unknown reasons. The present-day village of Cobá lies on either side of Lago Cobá, surrounded by dense jungle, 47 km inland from Tulum. It is a quiet, friendly village, with few tourists staying overnight.

The entrance to the ruins of this large but little-excavated city is at the end of the lake between the two parts of the village. A second lake, **Lago Macanxoc**, is within the site. There are turtles and many fish in the lakes, and it's a good birdwatching area. Both lakes and their surrounding forest can be seen from the summit of the **Iglesia**, the tallest structure in the **Cobá Group**. There are three other groups of buildings to visit: the **Macanxoc Group**, mainly stelae, about 1.5 km from the Cobá Group; **Las Pinturas**, 1 km northeast of Macanxoc, with a temple and the remains of other buildings that had columns in their construction; and the **Nohoch Mul Group**, at least another kilometre from Las Pinturas. Nohoch Mul has the tallest pyramid in the northern Yucatán, a magnificent structure, from which the views of the jungle on all sides are superb. You will not find at Cobá the great array of buildings that can be seen at Chichén Itzá or Uxmal, or the compactness of Tulum. Instead, the delight of the place is the architecture in the jungle, with birds, butterflies, spiders and lizards, and the many uncovered structures that hint at the vastness of the city in its heyday (the urban extension of Cobá is put at some 70 sq km). An unusual feature is the network of *sacbés* (sacred roads), which connect the groups in the site and are known to have extended across the entire Maya Yucatán. Over 40 *sacbés* pass through Cobá, some local, some of great length, such as the 100-km road to Yaxuná in Yucatán State.

At the lake, toucans may be seen very early; also look out for greenish-blue and brown mot-mots in the early morning. The guards at the site are very strict about opening and closing time so it is hard to get in to see the dawn or sunset from a temple.

The paved road into Cobá ends at **Lago Cobá**; to the left are the ruins, to the right **Villas Arqueológicas**. The roads around Cobá are badly potholed. Cobá is becoming more popular as a destination for tourist buses, which come in at 1030; arrive before that to avoid the crowds and the heat (ie on the 0430 bus from Valladolid, if not staying in Cobá). Take insect repellent.

Sian Ka'an Biosphere Reserve
Daily 0900-1500, 1800-2000, US$2. For information, visit Los Amigos de Sian Ka'an in Cancún, T998-892 2958, www.amigosdesiankaan.org; they are very helpful.

Meaning 'where the sky is born', the enormous reserve of Sian Ka'an, the third largest and one of the most diverse in all Mexico, was declared a UNESCO World Heritage Site in 1987 and now covers 652,000 ha (4500 sq km) of the Quintana Roo coast. About one-third is covered in tropical forest, one-third is savannah and mangrove, and one-third coastal and marine habitats, including 110 km of barrier reef. Mammals include jaguar, puma, ocelot and other cats, monkeys, tapir, peccaries, manatee and deer; turtles nest on the beaches; there are crocodiles and a wide variety of land and aquatic birds. If you want to see wildlife, it is best to use a qualified guide or tour operator (see Tour operators, below). You can drive into the reserve from Tulum village as far as Punta Allen (58 km; the road is opposite the turning to Cobá; it is not clearly marked and the final section is badly potholed), but beyond that you need a boat. Do not try to get there independently without a car.

Muyil
www.inah.gob.mx, 0800-1700, US$2.70.

The ruins of Muyil at **Chunyaxché** comprise three pyramids (partly overgrown) on the left-hand side of the road towards Felipe Carrillo Puerto, 18 km south of Tulum. One of the pyramids is undergoing reconstruction; the other two are relatively untouched. They are very quiet, with interesting birdlife, but also mosquito infested. Beyond the last pyramid is Laguna Azul, which is good for swimming and snorkelling in blue, clean water (you do not have to pay to visit the pool if you do not visit the pyramids).

Listings Tulum and around *map p57*

Where to stay

Tulum town
Scores of new budget hotels and restaurants are opening apace, making it a good base for backpackers and cost-conscious travellers. However, expect to offset those lower hotel rates with additional transport costs. There are no buses to the beach, only taxis and infrequent *colectivos*. For places to stay in Sian Ka'an Biosphere Reserve, see below.

$$$ Posada 6
Andrómeda Ote, between Gemini Sur and Satélite Sur, T984-116 6757, www.posada06tulum.com.
A stylish Italian-owned hotel with an interesting interior design that employs curves and enclaves to aesthetic effect. Rooms and suites are clean and comfortable, and amenities include garden, terraces, pool and jacuzzi.

$$$ Posada Luna del Sur
Luna Sur 5, T984-871 2984, www.posadalunadelsur.com.
An intimate downtown lodging with light, airy, elegantly attired rooms, all with crisp white linen. The owner, Tom, is very hospitable and attentive, with lots of useful knowledge on the area. Immaculately clean and comfortable,

and breakfast is included in the price. Recommended.

$$ Suites Nadet
Orion Norte by Polar Ote and Av Tulum.
The recently remodelled rooms at Suites Nadet are clean, simple and comfortable, all with smart new furnishings, a/c, hot water and cable TV. The suites (**$$$**) are much better and have kitchen and dining room. A good overall deal for the quality, cleanliness and location.

$ Hostel Sheck
Av Satelite Norte and Sagitario, T984-133 3992, www.hostelsheck.com.
A new, clean, laid-back hostel with a sociable. Mixed dorms only. The garden is lush and tranquil with inviting hammocks and seating areas, and amenities include a full-service bar and well-equipped industrial kitchen. Good cooked breakfast is included. Recommended for thrifty backpackers.

$ Posada Los Mapaches
Carretera Cancún–Chetumal, T984-871 2700, www.posadalosmapaches.com. 1.5 km north of the village, near the entrance to the ruins.
A very sweet and basic lodging bursting with colourful flowers. The rooms are clean and simple, with shared bath. Mother and son hosts, Chela and Joaquín, are helpful and hospitable. Complimentary bikes and breakfast included. Highly recommended.

Tulum beach
A plethora of lodgings run the length of the coast from Tulum ruins to the Sian Ka'an Biosphere reserve. There is little infrastructure beyond these hotels and it's best to reach them by taxi; official rates are posted on a sign at the rank in the village.

$$$$ Cabañas La Luna
Carretera Tulum–Boca Paila Km 6.5, T1-818-631 9824 (US reservations), www.cabanaslaluna.com.
Lots of love and care has gone into **La Luna**, a very popular and reputable boutique hotel with interesting and creative lodgings, including 9 themed *cabañas*, an ocean-view room, a garden suite and 2 villas. Stunning setting, great service and attention to detail.

$$$$-$$$ Nueva Vida de Ramiro
Carretera Tulum–Boca Paila Km 8.5, No 17, T984-877 8512, www.tulumnv.com.
Nueva Vida de Ramiro prides itself on attentive service and sustainable, ecologically aware practices. They offer luxury lodging in 30 wooden bungalows situated on a 7.5-ha beachfront property. Each unit boasts comfortable and tasteful furnishings, the height of rustic chic.

$$$$-$$$ Posada Margherita
T984-801 8493, www.posadamargherita.com.
There's a shabby-chic aesthetic at the **Posada Margherita**, with some furnishings made from reclaimed driftwood. The vibe is relaxed, the crowd trendy. A generally decent and hospitable lodging with 24-hr electricity and wheelchair access. Many people come for the excellent Italian food, but be warned, it's not cheap (**$$$**).

$$$ Dos Ceibas
9 km from the ruins, T984-877 6024, www.dosceibas.com.
This verdant ecolodge on the edge of the Sian Ka'an Biosphere Reserve has a range of comfortable and cheerful *cabañas*. Massage, cleansing rituals, New Age therapies and yoga instruction available. Friendly and tranquil ambience.

$$$-$$ Los Arrecifes
7 km from ruins, T984-155 2957, www. losarrecifestulum.com.
Clean, simple and affordable rooms and *cabañas*, a little tired, but with an excellent location on the beach and superb views of the ocean. The ambience is quiet and peaceful, the service adequate.

$$ Ahau Tulum
Carretera Tulum–Boca Paila Km 7.5, T984-167 1154, www.ahau tulum.com.
Named after the Mayan sun god, **Ahau Tulum** is a community-oriented resort with a New Age philosophy. They offer yoga, retreats and spa treatments. Recommended as one of the few reasonable budget beach options; rustic lodging is in the guesthouse. Asian-style *cabañas* are more expensive (**$$$-$$**), as are the luxurious suites (**$$$$**). Book in advance.

Cobá

$$ Hotelito Sac-Be
Calle Principal, 150 m from Town Hall.
Simple, clean, adequate rooms below a restaurant. Nothing outstanding, not great value, but the best available. Amenities include hot water and a/c. Friendly owner.

Sian Ka'an Biosphere Reserve

$$$$ Rancho Sol Caribe
Punta Allen, T984-139 3839, www. solcaribe-mexico.com.
Luxurious, extravagant and exclusive, **Rancho Sol Caribe** boasts a handful of handsome suites and *cabañas*, and an enviable location on the beach. Very hospitable and deeply relaxing, but not cheap. All-inclusive packages available. Recommended.

$$$ Centro Ecológico Sian Ka'an
T984-871 2499, www.cesiak.org.
Environmentally considerate and sensitive accommodation in the heart of the reserve, profits contribute to conservation and education programmes in the region. Tours, kayaking and fly fishing arranged.

Restaurants

Tulum town

$$$ El Pequeño Buenos Aires
Av Tulum, www.pequenobuenosaires.com.
High-quality cuts of beef, including rib eye, tenderloin, sirloin and more, all prepared and cooked to perfection the Argentine way. Cosy setting with open-air seating on the main drag. One great meat feast, the servings are large.

$$$ Ginger
Calle Polar between Av Satélite and Centauro, www.gingertulum.com.
A very decent, creative restaurant, if not the best in town. Starters include ceviche with mango and green apple and balsamic-glazed strawberry salad with goat cheese. For the main course, try the pan-seared fish fillet in passion fruit salsa or the grilled chicken in Yucatán spices. Recommended.

$$$ La Gloria de Don Pepe
Orion Sur 57.
An intimate little Spanish restaurant with just a few tables and a welcoming host. Authentic tapas, including *albóndigas* (meatballs) and *chistorra* (cured sausages), Catalan salads, tasty seafood paella, sangria and crisp white wine.

$$$-$$ La Malquerida
Calle Centauro Sur and Av Tulum.
A cheery Mexican restaurant serving tacos, fajitas, nachos, quesadillas and

the usual local fare, with a smattering of Caribbean and seafood. Large portions, friendly service and a laid-back, sociable ambience. A good stock of tequila.

$$ La Nave
Av Tulum.
A very popular Italian restaurant and pizzeria. Good, authentically Italian stone-baked pizzas and a lively atmosphere most evenings.

$$-$ El Gourmet
Av Tulum corner of Centauro Sur.
An Italian deli stocking good cheeses and cured hams, salami, olives and other treats. They do delicious panini and ciabatta sandwiches for picnics.

$ Doña Tinas
Good basic and cheap, in a grass hut at southern end of town. **El Mariachito** next door also does good, cheap and cheerful grub.

Ice cream parlours

La Flor de Michoacán
Av Tulum.
This ice cream parlour on the main drag offers a wide variety of flavoured cones (try the coconut), a refreshing antidote to the searing Caribbean heat.

Tulum beach

Restaurants on the beach tend to be owned by hotels. For dinner, book in advance where possible. Strolling between establishments after dark isn't advisable.

$$$ Mezzanine
Carretera Tulum–Boca Paila Km 1.5.
Excellent authentic Thai cuisine conceived by TV personality Chef Dim Geefay, who has successfully infused old family recipes with local, Mexican flavours. Specialities include pad thai and a host of flavourful curries. Highly recommended.

$$$ Restaurant Margherita
Carretera Tulum–Boca Paila Km 4.5, in Posada Margherita, www.posada margherita.com. Closed Sun.
Excellent, freshly prepared Italian food in an intimate setting. Hospitable, attentive service. Book in advance. Recommended.

$$$ La Zebra
Carretera Tulum–Boca Paila Km 7.5, www.lazebratulum.com.
Fresh, tasty barbequed fish, shrimps, ceviche and Mexican fare. Lashings of Margarita at the **Tequila Bar**.

$$$-$$ Restaurare
Carretera Tulum–Boca Paila Km 6.
Excellent vegan cuisine, healthy and flavourful, all served under the trees in a verdant jungle garden (bring repellent). Offerings include avocado soup, coconut curry and delicious fresh fruit juices. No alcohol served, bring your own if desired.

$$$-$$ Ziggy's
Carretera Tulum–Boca Paila Km 7, www.ziggybeachtulum.com.
Ziggy's serves seafood and vegetarian dishes, all creatively prepared with local ingredients. Offerings include mushroom ceviche, coconut shrimp and smoked pork chop and pineapple wrap. The sun loungers and *palapas* are part of the beach club.

What to do

Cenote diving
Koox Diving, *Av Tulum, between Osiris and Beta Norte, T984-131 6543, www.kooxdiving.com.* **Koox** is a friendly,

> **ON THE ROAD**
>
> ## Cenote diving
>
> There are more than 50 *cenotes* in this area – accessible from Ruta 307 and often well signposted – and cave diving has become very popular. However, it is a specialized sport and, unless you have a cave diving qualification, you must be accompanied by a qualified Dive Master.
>
> A cave diving course involves over 12 hours of lectures and a minimum of 14 cave dives using double tanks, costing around US$600. Accompanied dives start at around US$60. Specialist dive centres offering courses are: **Aquatech**, Villas de Rosa, PO Box 25, T984-875 9020, www.cenotes.com; **Aventuras Akumal No 35**, Tulum, T984-875 9030; **Aktun Dive Centre**, PO Box 119, Tulum, T984-871 2311; and **Cenote Dive Center**, Tulum, T984-876 3285, www.cenotedive.com.
>
> Two of the best *cenotes* are 'Carwash', on the Cobá road, good even for beginners, with excellent visibility; and 'Dos Ojos', just off Ruta 307 south of Aventuras, the second largest underground cave system in the world. It has a possible link to the Nohoch Nah Chich, the most famous *cenote* and part of a subterranean system recorded as the world's largest, with over 50 km of surveyed passageways connected to the sea.
>
> A word of warning: *cenote* diving has a higher level of risk than open-water diving – do not take risks and only dive with recognized operators.

personable and professional company with a solid team headed by Jesús 'Chucho' Guzmán. They offer reef and *cenote* dives, snorkel tours and certification up to Dive Master.
Xibalba Dive Center, *Andrómeda, between Libra and Gemini, T529-848 7129, www.xibalbahotel.com/diving.asp*. Headed by Robert Schmittner, **Xibalba** has been diving *cenotes* in the Yucatán for more than a decade. They visit around a dozen sites and offer PADI certification up to Dive Master, as well as NACD technical cave and cavern certification.

Kitesurfing
Extreme control, *El Paraíso Beach Club, T984-745 4555, www.extremecontrol.net*. Managed by Marco and Heather, **Extreme Control** is a very successful kiteboarding operation with branches across Mexico and Brazil. Basic lessons for groups start at US$60 per person. They also offer paddle-boarding and diving.

Tour operators
Community Tours Si'an Kaan, *Osiris Sur, between Sol Ote and Andrómeda Ote, T984-871 2202, www.siankaantours.org*. A socially responsible and environmentally aware tour operator entirely operated by Maya from local communities. They offer a range of professional cultural and adventure excursions, including wetland kayaking, birding and visits to *chicle* (chewing gum) farms.
Yucatán Outdoors, *T984-133 2334, www.yucatanoutdoors.com*. **Yucatán Outdoors** offers ecotourism

for adventurous souls, including personalized kayaking, hiking, birding and biking tours. Committed to sustainability and passionate about the local culture and environment.

Transport

Bicycle
Bikes can be hired in the village from **Iguana Bike Shop**, Calle Satélite Sur and **Andrómeda Ote**, T984-119 0836 (mob) or T984-871 2357.

Bus
Regular buses go up and down the coastal road travelling from Cancún to Tulum en route to Chetumal, stopping at most places in between. Some buses may be full when they reach Tulum; very few buses begin their journeys here.

To **Chetumal**, frequent departures, 4 hrs, 2nd class, US$14, 1st class US$17. To **Cobá**, mostly 2nd class, 1 hr, US$4. To **Escárcega**, ADO, 1825, 2300, 7 hrs, US$35. To **Felipe Carrillo Puerto**, frequent departures, 1½ hrs, US$6; also *colectivos* from the highway. To **Mérida**, ADO, 10 daily, 4 hrs, US$20; and numerous 2nd-class departures. To **Mexico City**, ADO, 1340, 23½ hrs, US$130. To **Palenque**, OCC, 1825, 2300, 10-11 hrs, US$52; and **ADO GL**, 2015, US$58. To **San Cristóbal**, OCC, 1825, 15 hrs, US$61; and an **ADO GL**, 2015, US$74. To **Villahermosa**, ADO, 4 daily, 11 hrs, US$54.

Taxi
Tulum town to Tulum **ruins** US$5.50. To the **beach** US$5.50 minimum, check the board by the taxi stand on Av Tulum for a full list of fixed rates. **Tucan Kin** run shuttles to Cancún airport, T01-800-702-4111 for reservations, www.tucankin.com, from US$29, 1½ hrs.

Cobá

Bus
Buses into the village turn round at the road end. To **Playa del Carmen**, ADO, 1510, 1530, 2 hrs, US$9. To **Tulum**, ADO, 1510, 1530, 1 hr, US$5.

Felipe Carrillo Puerto and around

The cult of the 'talking cross' started in Felipe Carrillo Puerto, a small town founded Chan Santa Cruz by Mayan rebels in 1850 (see box, page 66). The Santuario de la Cruz Parlante is five blocks west of the Pemex station on Highway 307. The beautiful main square is dominated by the Balam Nah Catholic church. Legend has it that the unfinished bell tower will only be completed when the descendants of those who heard the talking cross reassert control of the region.

Mahahual

Further south on Route 307, at Cafetal, a good road heads east to Mahahual (Majahual) on the coast (56 km from Cafetal), a peaceful place with clear water and beautiful beaches. Unfortunately, the Costa Maya cruise ship dock, 3 km from the village, means occasional interruptions to the peace and calm. From Mahahual, an offshore excursion is possible to **Banco Chinchorro**, where there is a coral bank and a white-sand beach. There is an ADO bus stop in Mahahual, but services from Cancún and Chetumal are quite infrequent.

Listings Felipe Carrillo Puerto and around

Where to stay

Felipe Carrillo Puerto

$$ Hotel Esquivel
Calle 65 No746, between 66 y 68, T983-834 0344, www.hotelesquivel.blogspot.mx.
The best in town, but simple. Rooms are clean and spacious, and include good hot water, a/c and Wi-Fi. Helpful service, close to the bus station, but perhaps not the best value.

$$-$ Chan Santa Cruz
Calle 68, 782, just off the plaza, T983-834 0021.
The 2nd best option, generally good, clean and friendly. Rooms have a/c, cable TV, fridge and disabled access.

Mahahual and around

$$$ El Hotelito
Av Mahahual, T983-834 5702, www.elhotelitomahahual.com.
A new, comfortable, tastefully decorated boutique hotel located at the southern end of the *malecón*, just across the street from the beach. Rooms on the top floor enjoy unobstructed ocean views and refreshing breezes. Good hosts and friendly, attentive service. Recommended.

$$$ Posada Pachamama
Huachinango s/n, T983-834 5762.
A homely little *posada* with clean, cosy, smallish rooms, modern conveniences and attractive decor. Italian owners Max and Michela are helpful and hospitable. Not quite on the beach, 1 min away, but most guests don't seem to mind. Recommended.

$$ Kabah-na
Camino Costero Mahahual–Xcalak Km 8.6, T983-838 8861, www.kabah na.com.
Simple, comfortable, relaxing beach *cabañas*, located several kilometres out of town, far from the hurly burly of the cruise ship crowds. Neither chic nor rustic, but somewhere in between. Best accessed with own vehicle.

Restaurants

Mahahual

$$$-$$ Tropicante
Av Mahahual, on the malecón, www.sandalsandskis.com/Tropicante.html.
Mexican and American food served on the beach. They have sun loungers too, if you prefer to simply rest up with a beer or cocktail. Note **Tropicante** often caters to the cruise ship crowd, so time your visit accordingly. Steve, the owner, is a good host.

$$ Pizza Papi
Av Paseo del Puerto.
Casual little Italian eatery serving very good, authentic, stone-baked pizzas. Good service. Recommended.

Transport

Felipe Carrillo Puerto
Bus
Bus station opposite Pemex. To **Cancún**, frequent 1st- and 2nd-class departures, 4 hrs, US$16. To **Chetumal**, frequent departures, 2½ hrs, US$10. To **Playa del Carmen**, frequent departures, 2½ hrs, US$11.50. To **Tulum**, frequent departures, 1½ hrs, US$7.50; also frequent *colectivo* minibuses.

ON THE ROAD
A brief history of the Caste War

Throughout the colonial era, the Yucatán enjoyed considerable independence from Mexico City, thanks to its geographic distance and its international trade. In the 19th century, as the capital relented to instability, the Yucatán enjoyed a prodigious economic boom fuelled by its expanding sugar and henequen (sisal) plantations.

But beyond the façade of urban gentrification, ethnic tensions festered in the countryside, especially when the sprawl of Yucatec haciendas began encroaching on communal Mayan lands. Against a backdrop of high taxes and shifting political transformations – independence from Spain, the emergence of a short-lived independent Yucatán, and its eventual incorporation into a federal Mexico – the Caste War broke out in 1847. Marred by atrocities on both sides, the conflict claimed 200,000 lives and very nearly resulted in an autonomous Mayan state.

The roots of the conflict lay far back in the Spanish conquest. In 1526, Francisco de Montejo and Alonso de Dávila were sent to conquer the Yucatán, but it was not until 1560 that the region fell decisively under the jurisdiction of the *audencia* of Mexico. Like other parts of New Spain, a strict racial hierarchy pervaded the colonial way of life: government was made up of Spanish-born upper classes only and based on the subordination of the *indígenas* and *mestizos*. In the same spirit, the prevailing *encomienda* system was tantamount to slavery, but it was soon replaced by the hacienda system with its feudal airs and absolute title to land. Christianization of the Yucatán intensified in 1571, the year of the Inquisition.

But despite the best efforts of the church to suppress Mayan culture – including those of Bishop Diego de Landa, who destroyed scores of Mayan

Chetumal and around
a small, non-touristy Mexican city with an authentic feel

The state capital of Quintana Roo, Chetumal, 240 km south of Tulum, is a necessary stopover for travellers en route to Mayan sites in the south of the peninsula and across the frontier to Belize and Guatemala; (see box, page 139). Although attractions are thin on the ground, Chetumal does have the advantage of being not devoted to tourism unlike other towns on the Riviera Maya. The Chetumal bay has been designated a natural protected area for manatees and includes a manatee sanctuary.

Sights
The avenues are broad, busy and in the centre lined with huge shops selling cheap imported goods. The main local activity is window-shopping and the atmosphere is more like a North American city, with an impression of affluence that can be a

idols and ancient manuscripts in a single day of religious zeal – the *indígenas* managed to preserve their customs and spiritual beliefs. Rebellions and armed uprisings against the Spanish Yucatecos were frequent, but none were as bloody and protracted as the Caste War.

During the conflict, the Maya received considerable military support from the British, who smuggled weapons into the region from their own colony in British Honduras. By 1848, having taken the entire peninsula except the cities of Campeche and Mérida, the Maya seemed poised for victory. What happened next is a matter of academic debate. Some historians claim that the Maya ran out of supplies and were forced to retreat. Another more poetic version recounts how the annual emergence of swarms of flying ants, a phenomenon traditionally signaling the onset of planting season, prompted the Maya to return to their beloved crops of maize.

Seizing the moment, the Yucatecos mounted a formidable counter-offensive with the help of the Mexican government and US mercenaries, driving the rebels into the southeastern corner of the peninsula. But the Maya, undaunted by their defeats and unfettered from Spanish oppression, soon declared their own independent state at the newly forged settlement of Noh Cah Santa Cruz Xbalam Nah, better known as Chan Santa Cruz (today, Felipe Carrillo Puerto), where a fervent religious revival had culminated in the 'cult of the talking cross' (the cross predated Christianity as a symbol of the Mayan World Tree).

Their military theocracy enjoyed some years of stability and autonomy, but sporadic skirmishes with the Yucatecos continued. The war officially ended when President Porfirio Díaz negotiated the border of British Honduras and the British agreed to stop supplying arms to the Maya. Soon after, General Ignacio Bravo was sent to stamp out any remaining dissent in the region. In 1901, he occupied Chan Santa Cruz, ending the experiment in Mayan autonomy.

culture shock to the visitor arriving from the much poorer country of Guatemala. The downtown area is compact and can be navigated on foot; Avenida Héroes is the main commercial thoroughfare.

The *paseo* near the waterfront on Sunday night is worth seeing. The State Congress building has a mural showing the history of Quintana Roo. The **Museo de la Cultura Maya** ⓘ *Av Héroes de Chapultepec by the market, Tue-Sun 0900-1900, US$5*, is highly recommended. It has good models of sites and touch-screen computers explaining the Mayan calendar and glyphs. Although there are few original Mayan pieces, it gives an excellent overview; some explanations are in English and guided tours are available.

Around Chetumal

Some 6 km north of Chetumal are the stony beaches of **Calderitas** (bus every 30 minutes from Colón, between Belice and Héroes, US$1.80, or taxi US$5) which has many fish restaurants. Beyond are the unexcavated archaeological sites of

Ichpaatun (13 km), **Oxtancah** (14 km) and **Nohochmul** (20 km). Sixteen kilometres north on Route 307 to Tulum is the **Laguna de los Milagros**, a beautiful lagoon for swimming. Further on, 34 km north of Chetumal, is **Cenote Azul**, over 70 m deep, with a waterside restaurant serving inexpensive and good seafood and regional food (but awful coffee) until 1800. Both the *laguna* and the *cenote* are deserted in the week.

Bacalar

About 3 km north of Cenote Azul is the village of Bacalar on the **Laguna de Siete Colores**, good for swimming and skin-diving; *colectivos* from terminal (Suchaa) in Chetumal, corner of Miguel Hidalgo and Primo de Verdad, 0700-1900 every 30 minutes, US$3, return from the plaza when full; also buses from Chetumal bus station every two hours or so, US$3. Built 1725-1733, the Spanish fort of **San Felipe** overlooks the shallow, clear, freshwater lagoon. It is a structure designed to withstand attacks by English pirates and smugglers who regularly looted Spanish galleons laden with Peruvian gold. Today, there are many old shipwrecks on the reef and around the Banco Chinchorro, 50 km out in the Caribbean. At the fort, there is a plaque praying for protection from the British and a small **museum** ⓘ *Tue-Sun 0900-1700, US$4*. There is a dock for swimming north of the plaza, with a restaurant and disco next to it.

Towards Campeche State

From Chetumal you can visit the fascinating Mayan ruins that lie west on the way (Route 186) to Francisco Villa and Escárcega, if you have a car. There are few tourists in this area and few facilities. Take plenty of drinking water. About 25 km from Chetumal at **Ucum** (where fuel is available), you can turn off 5 km south to visit **Palmara**, located along the Río Hondo, which borders Belize; there are swimming holes and restaurant.

Just before Francisco Villa (61 km from Chetumal), the ruins of **Kohunlich** ⓘ *0800-1700, US$4.25*, lie 8.5 km south of the main road, 1½ hours' walk along a sweltering, unshaded road; take plenty of water. Descriptions are in Spanish and English. Every hour or so the van passes for staff working at **Explorer Kohunlich**, a luxury resort hotel halfway to the ruins, which may give you a lift, but you'll still have 4 km to walk. There are fabulous masks (early Classic, AD 250-500) set on the side of the main pyramid, still bearing red colouring; they are unique of their kind (allow an hour for the site). About 200 m west of the turning for Kohunlich is an immigration office; wait here for buses to Chetumal or Xpujil, which have to stop, but first-class buses will not pick up passengers. *Colectivos* 'Nicolás Bravo' from Chetumal, or buses marked 'Zoh Laguna' pass the turning.

Other ruins in this area are **Dzibanché** and **Knichná** ⓘ *0900-1700, US$3.50*. Both are recent excavations and both are accessible down a dirt road off the Chetumal–Morocoy road. In the 1990s the remains of a Mayan king were disinterred at Dzibanché, which is thought to have been the largest Mayan city in southern Quintana Roo, peaking between AD 300 and 1200. Its discoverer, Thomas Gann, named it in 1927 after the Maya glyphs he found engraved on the sapodilla wood lintels in Temple VI – *Dzibanché* means 'writing on the wood' in Maya. Later excavations revealed a tomb in Temple I, believed to have belonged to a king because of the number of offerings it contained. This temple is also known as the **Temple of the Owl** because one of the artefacts unearthed was a vase and lid carved with an owl figure. Other important structures are the **Temple of the Cormorants** and **Structure XIII**, known as 'The Captives', due to its friezes depicting prisoners. Knichná means 'House of the Sun' in Maya, christened by Thomas Gann in reference to a glyph he found there. The **Acropolis** is the largest structure. To reach these sights follow the Chetumal–Escárcega road, turn off at Km 58 towards Morocoy, 9 km further on. The road to Dzibanché is 2 km down this road, crossing the turning for Knichná.

Listings Chetumal and around

Tourist information

Municipal tourist office
Corner of 5 de Mayo and Carmen Ochoa de Merino, T983-833 2465.
Stocks of maps and flyers, and enthusiastic staff.

Where to stay

$$$-$$ Los Cocos
Av Héroes de Chapultepec 134, T983-835 0430, www.hotelloscocos.com.mx.
A large, modern, professionally managed hotel with clean, comfortable rooms and suites, a good restaurant, decking and outdoor jacuzzi. Good value and popular, if a bit generic.

$$$-$$ Villanueva
Carmen Ochoa de Merino 166, T983-267 3370, www.hotel-villanueva.com.
A swish new business hotel with sparse contemporary furnishings and a wealth of facilities including pool, gym, business centre, restaurant and room service. Good value when promotions are available (**$$**).

$$ Hotel Gandhi
Av Gandhi 166, T983-285 3269, www.hotelgandhichetumal.com.
A step up from the bare-bones **Ucum** across the street, **Hotel Gandhi** is a reliable business hotel with clean, comfortable a/c rooms, complete with Wi-Fi, a/c and cable TV. Convenient for a night, but ultimately unremarkable.

$$-$ Paakal's Hostel
Av Juárez 364A, T983-833 3715.
Paakal's is a good, clean, friendly hostel with both private rooms ($$) and dorms ($), a well-equipped shared kitchen, lounge space, table tennis, plunge pool and relaxing garden. A newish property in excellent condition, very quiet and chilled out. Recommended for budget travellers.

$$-$ Ucum
Gandhi 167, corner of 16 de Septiembre, T983-832 6186.
Motel-style lodging with parking, centrally located and no frills. Rooms are ultra-basic, with a bed, a/c, hot water, Wi-Fi and cable TV. Charmless, but a good deal for thrifty wanderers.

Bacalar

$$$$ Akal Ki
Carretera Federal 307, Km 12.5, Bacalar Lagoon, T983-106 1751, www.akalki.com.
A marvellously peaceful retreat with romantic thatched bungalows built right over the water. Though surrounded by jungle, this strip of the lagoon has few rocks and little vegetation, making it crystal clear and ideal for swimming.

$$$ Rancho Encantado
3 km north of Bacalar, Carretera Federal 307, Km 24, on the west shore of the lagoon, T983-839 7900, www.encantado.com.
Comfortable, clean, spacious *cabañas*, suites and rooms, all in verdant surroundings by the lagoon. Services include private dock, tour boat, paddle boat, kayaks, restaurant and spa treatments.

$$ Casita Carolina
T983-834 2334, Costera 15, between Calle 16 and 18, www.casitacarolina.com.
Colourful, comfortable, good-value rooms at this friendly guesthouse, the best budget option in the village. The garden backs directly onto the lagoon and the plaza is just 2 blocks away. There are kayaks for rent, a shared kitchen and hammocks. Recommended.

Restaurants

$$$-$$ El Emporio
Merino 106.
Delicious Uruguayan steaks served in a historic old house near the bay. Popular with businessmen at lunchtime.

$$$-$$ Sergio's Pizza
Av Obregón 182.
A convenient downtown location for a popular family restaurant serving pizzas, fish and steaks. Good drinks and service, and a refreshing a/c interior. Very reasonable, but not amazing.

$$ La Casita del Chef
Obregón 163.
Featuring 100-year-old photos of Chetumal, **La Casita del Chef** is a pleasant little eatery serving traditional Mexican dishes with contemporary flair. Convenient downtown location and a traditional wooden building.

$$-$ Pasión Turca
Av Héroes and Ignacio Zaragoza, www.pasionturca.com.mx.
Chetumal is home to a large Turkish

community and the **Pasión Turca** is one of the best places to sample Turkish cuisine, with a Mexican twist, naturally. A simple place with slightly tired decor, but the food makes up for it.

$ Los Milagros
Zaragoza and 5 de Mayo.
This locals' café serves economical Mexican fare, *comida corrida* and breakfasts. Busy with patrons in the morning, worth a look.

$ Mercado
Cheap meals in the market at the top of Av Héroes, but the service is not too good and tourists are likely to be stared at. Lots of cheap *taquerías* on the streets nearby.

Bacalar

$ Los Hechizos
Hotel Rancho Encantado, Carretera Federal 307, www.encantado.com/restaurante.htm.
A rustic *palapa* with great views of the lagoon and refreshing breezes. Good food, the best in town, including a range of well-presented Mexican, seafood and meat dishes. Recommended.

Cafés

$ In Chiich
Calle 22, on the plaza.
Cute little café serving crêpes, smoothies, ice cream, snacks and good coffee.

Transport

For more information on crossing the border to Belize, see box, page 139.

Air
The airport (CTM), T983-834-5013, is 2.5 km from town. There are no local buses so take a taxi into town.

Flights to **Cancún**, **Mérida**, **Belize City**, **Mexico City**, **Monterrey** and **Tijuana**.

Boat
Boats from Belize dock at the pier on the waterfront on the south side of the city.

To Belize You can avoid a lot of the hassle of travelling overland to Belize, skipping Belize City altogether, by taking a boat from the Muelle Fiscal on the south side of the city, journey time 2 hrs (excluding immigration formalities). There are 2 companies, both with departures at 1500 to **San Pedro**, US$40, and on to **Caye Caulker**, US$45; fares rise by US$10 at weekends and holidays. Try **Water Jets International**, www.sanpedrowatertaxi.com, or **Belize Express Water Taxi**, T983-832 1648, www.belizewatertaxi.com. Buy tickets at least 24 hrs in advance.

Bus
The **ADO** bus terminal is 3 km out of town at the intersection of Insurgentes y Belice. Taxi into town US$2. There is a bus into the centre from Av Belice. 2nd-class buses from **Belize** arrive at the **Nuevo Mercado Lázaro Cárdenas**, on Calle Antonio Coria s/n, near the concrete tower in the market. Shuttles from **Santa Elena** and the border arrive at their own terminal, **Primo de Verdad**, between 16 de Septiembre and Hidalgo.

Bus information, T983-832 5110. At the ADO bus terminal left-luggage lockers cost US$0.30 per hr. If buying tickets in advance, go to the ADO office on Av Belice esq Gandhi, 0800-1600. There are often more buses than those marked on the display in the bus station, always ask at the information desk. Long-distance buses are often all booked a day ahead, so avoid unbooked connections. For local destinations in southern Quintana Roo, speedy minibuses depart from the terminal at Av Hidalgo and Primo de Verdad.

To **Bacalar**, very frequent 1st- and 2nd-class departures, 1 hr, US$3.50. To **Campeche**, **ADO**, 1200, 6 hrs, US$29. To **Cancún**, many 1st-class departures, 6 hrs, US$25. To **Escárcega**, **ADO**, 11 daily, 4 hrs, US$19. To **Felipe Carrillo Puerto**, many 1st- and 2nd-class departures, 2½ hrs, US$11. To **Mérida**, **ADO**, 5 daily, 5½ hrs, US$30. To **Palenque**, **OCC**, 0220, 2150, 7 hrs, US$32; and **ADO GL**, 2350, US$39. To **Playa del Carmen**, frequent 1st- and 2nd-class departures, 5 hrs, US$21. To **San Cristóbal**, **OCC**, 0220, 2150, 12 hrs, US$47; and **ADO GL** 0005, US$56. To **Tulum**, frequent 1st- and 2nd-class departures, 4 hrs, US$17. To **Villahermosa**, **ADO**, 6 daily, 8½ hrs, US$38. To **Xpujil**, **ADO**, **Sur** and **OCC**, 2 hrs, US$9.

To Belize Battered 2nd-class buses to Belize depart from a parking area in the Nuevo Mercado Lázaro Cárdenas, Calle Antonio Coria s/n, every 30-60 mins. To **Corozal**, 30-60 mins, US$1.50; to **Orange Walk**, 2 hrs, US$3.50; to **Belize City**, 3-4 hrs, US$5. Alternatively, if light on luggage, take a local bus to Santa Elena from the terminal on Primo de Verdad, between 16 de Septiembre and Hidalgo, 15 mins, US$0.80, cross the border on foot and pick up Belizean transport on the other side. Taxi from downtown Chetumal to the border, US$6. Money-changers in the bus terminal offer marginally poorer rates than those at the border. If intending to stay in Belize City, do not take a bus that arrives at night as you are advised not to look for a hotel in the dark.

To Guatemala San Juan Travel Services provide 1 daily service between Chetumal, Belize City and **Flores** in Guatemala, departs from **ADO** bus terminal 0700, US$31. Schedules are subject to change so always check times in advance, and be prepared to spend a night in Chetumal if necessary.

Taxi
There are no city buses; taxis run on fixed-price routes, US$1.50 on average. Cars with light-green licence plates are a form of taxi.

Yucatán State

Yucatán State is a vivid celebration of Yucatecan history and traditions: its wealth of cathedrals, convents and rambling haciendas, frequently set against a backdrop of crumbling Mayan pyramids, recall the passion and drama of another age.

The state capital of Mérida was the seat of power for the colonial administration. Today, it is a deeply cultural place filled with museums, theatres and art galleries, teeming markets and plazas, historic mansions, churches and bright townhouses. The city of Valladolid, although much smaller, is no less romantic.

Beyond its urban centres, the state is peppered with bucolic towns and villages, many rich in Mayan heritage and specializing in artesanía, while communities on the Convent Route are so called for their ancient religious architecture.

As the once-thriving heart of the Mayan world, the Yucatán State is also home to the vast city of Chichén Itzá, laden with sculpted feathered serpents and pyramids, ball courts and sacrificial slabs, a tremendous monument to an ancient culture. It is also worth exploring Uxmal, a stunning example of sumptuous Puuc-style architecture. Yucatán State has natural attractions too, including mysterious limestone cave systems and refreshing cenotes. On the coast, the wetlands Río Lagartos and Celestún are places to observe pelicans, egrets and flamingos.

Mérida

bold colonial buildings in varying states of repair

Mérida, the cultural and intellectual capital of the Yucatán Peninsula, is a bustling, tightly packed city. There is continual activity in the centre, with a huge influx of tourists during the high season mingling with busy *Meridanos* going about their daily business. Although the city has been developed over many years for tourism, there is plenty of local flavour, including the pungent and warren-like city market, a throng of commotion, noise and colour. Whether sipping coffee in a leafy colonial courtyard or admiring the mansions on the regal Paseo de Montejo, much of the pleasure in Mérida comes from exploring its architecture, a rich blend of European styles that spans the centuries. In the evenings, there is usually open-air dancing, music or singing. It is perhaps no surprise that many inhabitants of Mexico City are now relocating to the infinitely more civilized and urbane destination of Mérida.

You can see most of Mérida on foot. Although the city is big, there is not much to see outside the blocks radiating from the Plaza Grande; it is bound by Calles 60, 61, 62 and 63. The city centre is laid out in a classic colonial grid with even-numbered streets running north–south, odd-numbered east–west.

Plaza Grande and around

The city revolves around the large, shady Plaza Grande, site of the **cathedral**, completed in 1559, the oldest cathedral in Latin America, which has an impressive baroque façade. It contains the Cristo de las Ampollas (Christ of the Blisters), a statue carved from a tree that burned for a whole night after being hit by lightning, without showing any damage at all. Placed in the church at Ichmul, it suffered only a slight charring (hence the name) when the church was burned to the ground. To the left of the cathedral on the adjacent side of the plaza is the **Palacio de Gobierno**, built 1892. It houses a collection of 27 enormous murals by Fernando Castro Pacheco, depicting the bloody struggle of the Maya to integrate with the Spanish. The murals can be viewed until 2100 every day. The **Casa de Montejo** ⓘ *www.casasdeculturabanamex.com, Tue-Sun 1000-1900, Sun 1000-1400, free*, is on the south side of the plaza, a 16th-century palace built by the city's founder, today a branch of Banamex and a minor art museum. It features elaborate stonework above the doorway flanked by statues of conquistadors standing victorious on the necks of their (presumably Maya) enemies.

Away from the main plaza along Calle 60 is **Parque Hidalgo**, a charming tree-filled square, which borders the 17th-century **Iglesia de Jesús.** A little further along Calle 60 is the **Teatro Peón Contreras**, built at the beginning of the 20th century by an Italian architect, with a neoclassical façade, marble staircase and Italian frescoes.

Churches

There are several 16th- and 17th-century churches dotted about the city: **La Mejorada**, behind the Museum of Peninsular Culture (Calle 59 between 48 and

Mérida

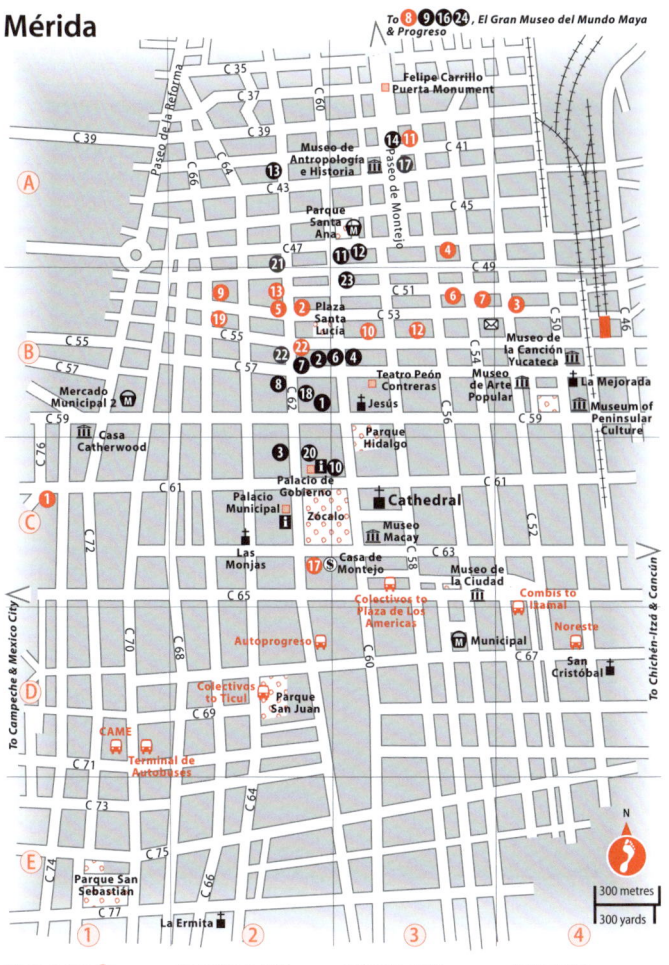

To 8 9 16 24, El Gran Museo del Mundo Maya & Progreso

Where to stay
Aventura Hotel 1 *C1*
Casa Alvarez 2 *B2*
Casa Ana 3 *B4*
Casa Lecanda 4 *A3*
Hacienda Mérida VIP 5 *B2*
Hacienda Xcanatún 8 *A3*
Hostal Zócalo 17 *C2*
Hotel del Pelegrino 6 *B3*
Julamis 7 *B3*
Los Arcos 9 *B2*
Luz en Yucatán 10 *B3*
Medio Mundo 19 *B2*
Nómadas Youth Hostal 13 *B2*
Rosas and Xocolate Boutique 11 *A3*
Santa María 12 *B3*
Trinidad 22 *B2*

Restaurants
Amaro 1 *B2*
Bistro Rescoldos 13 *A2*
Café Chocolate 23 *B3*
Café El Hoyo 7 *B2*
Cafetería Pop 2 *B2*
Casa de Piedra 24 *A3*
Chile Habanero 6 *B3*
El Colón Sorbetes y Dulces Finos 10 *C3*
El Nuevo Tucho 4 *B3*
El Trapiche 3 *C2*
La Chaya 8 *B2*
La Recova 9 *A3*
Manjar Blanco 11 *A3*
Marlín Azul 18 *B2*
Mérida 20 *C2*
Pizzeria Raffaello 12 *A3*
Rosas and Xocolate 14 *A3*
Trotter's 16 *A3*

Bars & clubs
Cantina La Negrita 21 *A2*
Hennessy's Irish Pub 17 *A3*
Mayan Pub 22 *B2*

Cancún & Yucatán Peninsula Yucatán State • 75

50), **Tercera Orden**, **San Francisco** and **San Cristóbal** (beautiful, in the centre). The **Ermita**, an 18th-century chapel with beautiful grounds, is a lonely, deserted place, 10 to 15 minutes from the centre.

Paseo de Montejo

Attempts to create a sophisticated Champs Elysées-style boulevard in the north of the city at Paseo Montejo have not been quite successful; the plan almost seems to go against the grain of Mérida's status as an ancient city, which has gradually evolved into a place with its own distinct identity. Nonetheless, the *paseo*, which is the principal parade route during the city's fantastic carnival celebrations, features numerous impressive mansions dating to the late 19th century. You can take a casual stroll or hire a horse-drawn carriage and do it in style. For a glimpse of the *paseo* at its heyday, the **Casa Museo Montes Molina** ⓘ *Paseo de Montejo No 469 between Calles 33 and 35, www.laquintamm.com, English tours Mon-Fri 0900, 1100, 1500, Sat 0900, 1100; Spanish tours Mon-Fri 1000, 1200, 1400, 1600, Sat 1000, 1200, US$4*, is a finely attired mansion with sumptuous antiques and art deco pieces.

Museums and art galleries

Mérida's wealth of museums is enough to keep most visitors busy for a few days. The **Museo Regional de Antropología** ⓘ *Paseo de Montejo 485, Tue-Sun 0800-1700, US$3.70*, housed in the beautiful neoclassical Palacio Cantón, has a collection of Mayan crafts and changing anthropological exhibits. However, most of its archaeological pieces have now been relocated to the Gran Museo del Mundo Maya (see below).

The **Museo de la Ciudad** ⓘ *Calle 56 between Calles 65 and 65-A, Tue-Fri 0900-2000, Sat 0900-1400, free*, has modest visual exhibits outlining the history of the city. The **Museo Macay** ⓘ *Calle 60, on the main plaza, www.macay.org, daily 1000-1800, free*, has a permanent exhibition of Yucatec artists, with temporary exhibits by contemporary local artists.

The **Museo de Arte Popular** ⓘ *Calle 50-A No 487 and Calle 57, Tue-Sat 0900-1700, Sun 1000-1500, free*, has a permanent exhibition of Mayan art, handicrafts and clothing, with a good souvenir shop attached. In the Casa de Cultura, the **Museo de la Canción Yucateca** ⓘ *Calles 57 and 48, Tue-Fri 0900-1700, Sat-Sun 0900-1500, US$1.50*, has an exhibition of objects and instruments relating to the history of music in the region. For contemporary painting and sculpture, head to the **Pinacoteca Juan Gamboa Guzmán** ⓘ *Calle 59, between Calles 58 and 60, Tue-Sat 0900-1700, Sun 1000-1700, US$2.40*.

Established in 2007, the **Galería de Arte Municipal** ⓘ *Calle 56, between Calles 65 and 65-A, Tue-Fri 1000-1900, Sun 1000-1400*, exhibits and promotes work by local Meridano artists. **Galería Tataya** ⓘ *Calle 60 No 409, between Calles 45 and 47, www.tataya.com.mx, Mon-Fri 1000-1400 and 1600-2000, Sat 1000-1400*, is a private gallery specializing in Mexican and Cuban contemporary art and high-quality *artesanías*. Dedicated exclusively to local artists, **Galería Mérida** ⓘ *Calle 59 No 452, between Calles 52 and 54, Tue-Fri 1000-1230 and 1430-1700, www.galeriamerida.com*, is a small gallery featuring a range of fine and contemporary art; exhibits change monthly.

BACKGROUND
Mérida

Mérida was originally a large Mayan city called Tihoo. It was conquered on 6 January 1542, by Francisco de Montejo. He dismantled the pyramids of the Maya and used the stone as the foundations for the cathedral of San Ildefonso, built 1556-1559. For the next 300 years, Mérida remained under Spanish control, unlike the rest of Mexico, which was governed from the capital. During the Caste Wars of 1847-1855, Mérida held out against the marauding forces of indigenous armies, who had defeated the Mexican army in every other city in the Yucatán Peninsula except Campeche. Reinforcements from the centre allowed the Mexicans to regain control of their city, but the price was to relinquish control of the region to Mexico City.

Railway fanatics might get some joy in the **Museo de los Ferrocarriles** ⓘ *Calle 43 between Calles 46 and 58, Col Industrial, Wed-Sun 0900-1400, US$1.50*, but there's little for the casual visitor. Fans of John Lloyd Steven's seminal travelogue *Incidents of Travel in Central America, Chiapas and Yucatán* should check out **Casa Catherwood** ⓘ *Calle 59 between 72 and 74, www.casa-catherwood.com, Mon-Sat 0900-1400 and 1700-2100, US$5*. Dedicated to Steven's companion and illustrator, Mr Catherwood, this museum contains stunning colour lithographs of Mayan ruins, as they were found in the 19th century.

★ El Gran Museo del Mundo Maya

Paseo Montejo and Calle 60, on the outskirts of the city, www.granmuseodelmundomaya.com, Wed-Mon 0800-1700, closed Tue, US$11.50; buses to the museum depart from the corner of Plaza Grande, Calle 62 and 61, check with the driver first, US$0.70, or take a taxi, US$5.50. To return to the city centre, take a bus from directly outside the museum.

Mérida's Gran Museo Mundo Maya is a state-of-the-art interactive museum dedicated to Mayan history and identity. Opened in 2012, its collection of 1160 cultural and archaeological pieces are supplemented by scores of touch screens, computers, projection rooms and a full-sized cinema. The museum has one temporary exhibition wing and a permanent collection wing with four main sections. The first section deals with the geographic and social landscape of the Yucatán, its ethnic and ecological diversity, its various territories, forms of social organization and languages. The second section is a detailed exploration of the Yucatán's present-day economy and culture, including exhibitions on education, health, tradition and work. The colonial era is the theme of the third section with an array of antiques and old machines relating to the colonial industries, the conquest, the church and Mayan rebellions. The fourth and final section hosts an impressive array of archaeological pieces from statues depicting Mayan deities to examples of Mayan hieroglyphs. It explores the ancient Mayan world through the diverse themes of cosmovision, art, architecture, astronomy, time and more.

Around Mérida

birdwatching, beaches and Mayan ruins

Celestún

A small, dusty fishing resort west of Mérida much frequented in summer by Mexicans, Celestún stands on the spit of land separating the Río Esperanza estuary from the ocean. The long beach is relatively clean except near the town proper, with clear water ideal for swimming, although rising afternoon winds usually churn up silt and there is little shade. Along the beach are many fishing boats bristling with *jimbas* (cane poles), used for catching local octopus. There are beach restaurants with showers.

The immediate region is a biosphere reserve, created to protect the thousands of migratory waterfowl who inhabit the lagoons; fish, crabs and shrimp also spawn here, and kingfishers, black hawks, wood storks and crocodiles may sometimes be glimpsed in the quieter waterways. In the winter months Celestún plays host to the largest flamingo colony in North America, perhaps more than 20,000 birds – in the summer most of the flamingos leave Celestún for their nesting grounds in the Río Lagartos area. Boat trips to view the wildlife can be arranged at the beach or the **visitor centre** ⓘ *below the river bridge 1 km back along the Mérida road, US$100 for 1-6 people, plus US$4 per person for the reserve entrance fees, 1½ hrs*. Make sure your boatman takes you through the mangrove channel and to the Baldiosera freshwater spring in addition to visiting the flamingos. It is often possible to see flamingos from the bridge early in the morning and the road to it may be alive with egrets, herons and pelicans. January to March is the best time to see them. It's important to wear a hat and use sunscreen. There are hourly buses to Mérida's terminal at Calle 50 and 67, 0530-2000, two to three hours, US$5.

Progreso and around

Some 36 km north of Mérida, Progreso has the nearest beach to the city. It is a port and slow-growing resort town, with the facilities improving to service the increasing number of US cruise ships that arrive every Wednesday. Progreso is famous for its industrial pier, which at 6 km is the longest in the world. It has been closed to the public since someone fell off the end on a moped. The beach is long and clean and the water is shallow and good for swimming.

A short bus journey (4 km) west from Progreso are **Puerto Yucalpetén** and **Chelem**. Balneario Yucalpetén has a beach with lovely shells, but also a large naval base with further construction in progress.

Some 5 km east of Progreso is another resort, **Chicxulub**; it has a narrow beach, quiet and peaceful, on which are many boats and much seaweed. Small restaurants sell fried fish by the *ración*, or kilogram, served with tortillas, mild chilli and *cebolla curtida* (pickled onion). Chicxulub is reputed to be the site of the crater made by a meteorite crash 65 million years ago, which caused the extinction of the dinosaurs. (The site is actually offshore on the ocean floor.) The beaches on this coast are often deserted and, between December and February, 'El Norte' wind blows in every 10 days or so, making the water turbid and bringing in cold, rainy weather.

Dzibilchaltún

0800-1700, US$9. Combis to the ruins depart from Calle 58 between Calles 59 and 57.

Halfway between Mérida and Progreso turn right for the Mayan ruins of Dzibilchaltún. This unique city, according to carbon dating, was founded as early as 1000 BC. The site is in two halves, connected by a *sacbé* (sacred road). The most important building is the **Templo de Las Siete Muñecas** (Temple of the Seven Dolls), at the east end, which is partly restored. At the west end is the ceremonial centre with temples, houses and a large plaza in which the open chapel, simple and austere, sticks out like a sore thumb. The evangelizing friars had clearly hijacked a pre-Conquest sacred area in which to erect a symbol of the invading religion. At its edge is the **Cenote Xlaca** containing very clear water that is 44 m deep (you can swim in it, take mask and snorkel as it is full of fascinating fish); there's a very interesting nature trail starting halfway between the temple and the *cenote*; the trail rejoins the *sacbé* halfway along. The **museum** is at the entrance by the ticket office (site map available). *Combis* stop here en route to **Chablekal**, a village along the same road.

South to Campeche State

South of the city, 18 km away, the first place of any size is **Umán**, a henequen- (sisal-) processing town with a large 17th-century church and convent dedicated to St Francis of Assisi; there are many *cenotes* in the flat surrounding limestone plain. Further south, a turn-off leads to the turn-of-the-20th-century Moorish-style henequen hacienda at **San Bernardo**, one of a number in the state that can be visited; an interesting museum chronicling the old Yucatán Peninsula tramway system is located in its spacious grounds. At **Maxcanú**, the road to Muná and Ticul branches east; a short way down it is the recently restored Mayan site of **Oxkintoc** ⓘ *US$3*. The Pyramid of the Labyrinth can be entered (take a torch) and there are other ruins, some with figures. Ask for a guide at the village of Calcehtoc, which is 4 km from the ruins and from the Grutas de Oxkintoc (no bus service). These, however, cannot compare with the caves at Loltún or Balankanché (see pages 90 and 98).

Listings Mérida and around *map p75*

Tourist information

It's worth getting hold of a copy of the excellent free tourist magazine, *Yucatan Today*, www.yucatantoday.com, published monthly and packed with useful information about the state and its attractions. Online, *Yucatán Living*, www.yucatanliving.com, is an informative expat site with news, reviews and current events.

Municipal tourist office
Calle 62, between Calles 61 and 63, T999-942 0000, www.yucatan.travel.
In the Palacio Municipal on the Plaza Grande, this main municipal tourist office is helpful and well stocked with maps and flyers; additional modules are in the Museo de Ciudad, TAME Terminal and the Paseo Montejo.

State tourist office
Calles 60 and 62, T999-930 3101, www.yucatan.travel.
In the Palacio de Gobierno, also on the Plaza Grande, with additional branches in the Teatro José Peón Contreras and the airport.

Where to stay

Mérida
If booking into a central hotel, always try to get a room away from the street side, as noise on the narrow streets begins as early as 0500.

$$$$ Casa Lecanda
Calle 47 No 471, between Calle 54 and 56, T999-928 0112, www.casalecanda.com.
Recalls the beauty and elegance of a traditional Meridano home with handsome interior patios and gardens. It has 7 rooms, all impeccably attired and luxurious.

$$$$ Hacienda Mérida VIP
Calle 62 No 441A, between Calle 51 and 53, T999-924 4363, www.hotelhaciendamerida.com.
An elegant art deco townhouse in the Centro Histórico, complete with pool, spa and parking. Boutique rooms have all modern amenities, artistic and tasteful furnishings, and luxurious touches such as Egyptian cotton sheets.

$$$$ Hacienda Xcanatún
Carretera Mérida–Progreso Km 12, 10 mins out of town, T999-930 2140, www.xcanatun.com.
A very elegant and carefully restored former henequen hacienda. They boast 18 sumptuous suites, spa facilities and one of the best restaurants in Mérida. Luxurious and romantic.

$$$$ Rosas & Xocolate Boutique Hotel & Spa
Paseo de Montejo No 480 and Calle 41, T999-924 2992, www.rosasandxocolate.com.
A stylish and romantic lodging with smart rooms in shades of pink, superb contemporary decor that echoes the traditional Yucatec style, excellent restaurant, and spa facilities. This boutique hotel would suit couples and hip young things.

$$$ Los Arcos
Calle 66 No 448-B, between Calle 53 and 49, T999-926 0145, www.losarcosmerida.com.
Classically elegant, **Los Arcos** is a 19th-century colonial house converted to an intimate B&B. It has rooms with high ceilings, fantastic displays of folk art and antiques, swimming pool and verdant garden. Friendly, personable service.

$$$ Medio Mundo
Calle 55 No 533 between Calle 64 and 66, T999-924 5472, www.hotelmediomundo.com.
Renovated old home now a charming classically Yucatec hotel with 12 tasteful, high-ceilinged rooms, lush garden patio and pool. Friendly, pleasant and quaint. Nice handicraft shop forms part of the hotel.

$$$-$$ Julamis
Calle 53 No 475B and Calle 54, T999-924 1818, www.hoteljulamis.com.
An award-winning B&B with stylish high-ceilinged rooms and a superb rooftop terrace, great for sipping tequila after dusk. Owner, Alex, is Swiss and a good host. A generous breakfast is included in the rates.

$$$-$$ Luz en Yucatán
Calle 55 No 499, between Calle 60 and 58, T999-924 0035, www.luzenyucatan.com.
A very welcoming, relaxed and slightly quirky 'urban retreat' with a range of comfortable rooms, studios and apartments. All have a contemporary look and good furnishings, including fridge. Outside, there's a pool and chilled-out garden. Interestingly, nightly rates vary according to your ability to pay, so those of modest means can stay too.

$$ Casa Alvarez
Calle 62 No 448 and Calle 53, T999-924 3060, www.casaalvarezguesthouse.com.
A pleasant, little guesthouse with a small pool and comfortable rooms, all well equipped with TV, a/c and other modern amenities. Family-run and friendly.

$$ Casa Ana
Calle 52 No 469, T999-924 0005, www.casaana.com.
A sweet little B&B with 5 rooms (a/c costs extra) and a family atmosphere, tropical garden and a small pool. Homely and quaint.

$$ Hotel del Pelegrino
Calle 51 No 488, between Calle 54 and 56, T999 924-3007, www.hoteldelperegrino.com.
This remodelled colonial house with its original tile work has 14 rooms, all different and very clean, and a outdoor terrace with a jacuzzi that's accessible at all hours. A small, friendly, family-run place, helpful and good value.

$$ Hotel Santa María
Calle 55 No 493, between Calle 58 and 56, T923-6512, www.hotelsantamariamerida.com.
A bit generic and uninspiring, but rooms are spacious, comfortable and fully equipped with cable TV, a/c and hot water. Pleasant lobby and a small pool. Modern and good value.

$$-$ Trinidad
Calle 62 No 464 esq 55, T999-923 2033, www.hotelestrinidad.com.
A bit dishevelled, but irresistibly bohemian. The lightly crumbling courtyard features trees, art work and signs reading 'don't feed the possum'. Friendly owners, a range of rooms, some much better (and more pricey) than others, the cheapest have shared bathroom. There's a 2nd **Hotel Trinidad** with a pool. Bring mosquito repellent.

$ Aventura Hotel
Calle 61 No 580, between Calle 74 and 76, T999-923 4801, www.aventurahotelmerida.com.
Small, simple, basic rooms along a leafy outside corridor, peaceful, 5-min walk from the centre, well-kept and clean, excellent value with a/c, hot water, cable TV and Wi-Fi.

$ Hostal Zócalo
On the south of the plaza, T999-930 9562, www.hostalzocalo.com.
Popular hostel with economical rooms and clean dormitories. There's TV, DVD, kitchen, laundry, chilled-out balconies and sunny terraces, tours and Wi-Fi. Full breakfast buffet included with the private rooms. Friendly management and good location.

$ Nómadas Youth Hostal
Calle 62 No 433, end of Calle 51, 5 blocks north of the plaza, T999-924 5223, www.nomadastravel.com.
A sociable hostel with private rooms and dorms. General services include hot water, full kitchen, drinking water, hammocks, swimming pool and internet. Owner Raúl speaks English and is very helpful. Good value and a

great place to meet other travellers. Lots of activities, including salsa, trova music, yoga and cooking classes. Bring mosquito repellent.

Celestún
Most lodgings are along Calle 12.

$$$$ Hotel Xixim
Km 10 off the old Sisal Hwy, T988-916 2100, www.hotelxixim.com.
Tranquil luxury bungalows and suites in a coconut grove on the edge of the beach and the reserve. They offer spa facilities, yoga, bicycles, kayaks, pool, and ecotours to surrounding area including flamingos, turtle nesting, etc.

$$ Gutiérrez
Calle 13 s/n, between Calles 12 and 14, T988-916 2609.
Modest and functional hotel on the beach. Rooms on top floor get ocean views and breezes. Amenities include Wi-Fi, patio and restaurant. Check the room and bed before accepting.

Progreso and around

$$ Hotel Quinta Progreso
Calle 23 No 64-C, between Calles 48 and 50, 600 m from the malecón, T969-934 4414, www.hotelquinta progreso.com.
A handsome colonial building with beautiful tile work and large, clean, tastefully decorated rooms. Amenities include swimming pool and tea bar. Prices include breakfast. Recommended.

$ Hostel Progreso
Calle 21 and 54, T969-103 0294, www.hostelprogreso.com.
This budget hostel is housed by an impressive 2-storey restored mansion 2 blocks from the *malecón*. It has dorm beds and simple private rooms, shared kitchen, ocean-facing decks, hammocks, and breakfast included.

Restaurants

There are a number of taco stands, pizzerias and sandwich places in Pasaje Picheta, a small plaza off the Palacio de Gobierno.

$$$ Casa de Piedra
Hacienda Xcanatún, Calle 20 s/n, Carretera Mérida–Progreso Km 12.
Live music Fri-Sat. Inside an old machine room with high ceiling, this award-winning restaurant serves French-Yucatec fusion, creative appetizers and mains, local seafood and meat. The place for a very romantic dinner or special occasion.

$$$ La Recova
Paseo de Montejo No 382, T999-944 0215, www.larecovamerida.com.
A popular Argentine steakhouse serving all certified 'Aberdeen Angus' and Kobe beef, huge cuts of meat, burgers and seafood. Modern and elegant interior, smart-casual and often busy. A good stock of wine.

$$$ Rosas and Xocalate
Paseo de Montejo No 480 and Calle 41, T999-924 2992, www.rosasandxocolate.com.
The place for a romantic candlelit dinner. They serve fusion cuisine by chef David Segovia, including courgette salad, catch of the day and chocolate tart, among other treats. Try the 6-course taster menu. Elegant, creative and interesting.

$$$ Trotter's
Circuito Colonias, between Paseo Montejo and Calle 60 Norte, www.trottersmerida.com.
Stylish steakhouse with a good wine list

and a mouth-watering array of Angus steaks, fresh fish and tapas. Includes a smart wine bar and great ambience in the romantic garden. Classy place, sophisticated. Take a taxi.

$$$-$$ Bistro Rescoldos
Calle 62 No 366, between Calles 41 and 43, T999-286 1028, www.rescoldosbistro.com.
Bistro Rescoldos, meaning 'burning embers', serves flavourful Italian and Greek cuisine with love, including falafels, hummus, tzatziki, calzones and wood-fired pizzas. Lovely outdoor patio, wonderful atmosphere. Recommended.

$$$-$$ Chile Habanero
Calle 60 No 483B, www.elchilehabanerorestaurante.com.
Good clean place with attentive staff, pleasant evening atmosphere and art work on the walls. Recommended for its Yucatec specialities, including *pollo pibil* and a good sample platter *delicias de Yucatán*. Pizzas look good, also does hamburgers.

$$$-$$ La Chaya
Calle 62 and 57, www.lachayamaya.com.
A famous and massively popular restaurant specializing in Yucatec dishes such as *poc chuc* and *pollo pibil*. Tortillas are prepared in front of diners and waitresses wear traditional clothes. Often busy and buzzing with locals and fun. Another branch on Calle 55, between Calles 60 and 62, is a larger and more atmospheric building with antique carriage, often serving big tour groups.

$$ Amaro
Calle 59 No 507 between Calle 60 and 62, near the plaza. Open late daily.
Good vegetarian food served in an open courtyard and covered patio. Try *chaya* drink from the leaf of the *chaya* tree; their curry, avocado pizza and home-made bread are also very good.

$$ El Nuevo Tucho
Calle 60 near University.
Local dishes, mostly meat and fish, and an extensive drinks menu. A rousing locals' joint, good fun place in the evenings, often with live music. Give it a go.

$$ Manjar Blanco
Calle 47 between Calles 58 and 60.
A very pleasant family-run restaurant with a smart, clean interior. Friendly service, Yucatec specialities and 'grandmother's authentic recipes'.

$$ Pizzeria Raffaello
Calle 60 440A.
Italian-style thin-crust pizzas, many to choose from, stone-baked in an oven outside. There's seating in the garden or casual dining indoors. Relaxed place, friendly owner, good service and pizzas.

$ Cafetería Pop
Calle 57, between Calles 60 and 62.
Low-key café attached to a hotel, they serve Mexican staples and international fare, breakfast, lunch and dinner. The *pollo con mole poblano* (chicken in chocolate and chilli sauce) is good. Clean and casual.

$ El Trapiche
Calle 62 half a block north of the plaza.
Sizzling spit of meat outside, hearty specials at lunchtime and economical grub à la carte. Staff are very friendly. Reasonable and cheap food, usually good. Sometimes a fun atmosphere in the evenings. Unpretentious.

$ Marlín Azul
Calle 62, between Calle 57 and 59.
Looks like a grotty hole in the wall, but there's an a/c section next door.

Amazing fresh seafood, including fileted catch of the day and ceviche, very simple and delicious, completely local. Recommended for a quick, casual lunch.

$ Mérida
Calle 62 between Calle 59 and 61.
This restaurant has been in Mérida for at least 10 years, always cheap and reliable, and now with an attractive remodelled interior and smartly attired waiters. Breakfast and lunch specials are popular with office workers. They serve simple Yucatec and Mexican food, not bad.

Cafés and ice cream parlours

Café Chocolate
Calle 60 No 442 y Calle 49, T999-928 5113, www.cafe-chocolate.com.mx.
In addition to coffee, this café and art space does good *mole*, an economical breakfast buffet, a lunchtime menu and evening meals. Cosy and bohemian, free Wi-Fi, sofas indoors or outdoor courtyard seating.

Café El Hoyo
Calle 62, between Calle 57 and 59.
Chilled-out tea house serving refreshing fruit and herbal infusions, coffee too, good sandwiches. Literature, board games.

El Colón Sorbetes y Dulces Finos
Calle 61 and 60, on the plaza.
Serving ice cream since 1907, great sorbets, *meringue*, good menu with explanation of fruits in English. About 30 different flavours of delicious ice cream.

Celestún
Many beachside restaurants along Calle 12, but be careful of food in the cheaper ones; recommended is **La Playita**, for simple fried fish, seafood cocktails. Food stalls along Calle 11 beside the bus station should be approached with caution.

$ Chivirico
Across the road from La Playita.
Offers descent fish, shrimp and other seafood.

$$ El Lobo
Calle 10 and 13, on the corner of the main square.
Best spot for breakfast, with fruit salads, yoghurt, pancakes, etc. Celestún's best pizza in the evenings.

Progreso and around
The *malecón* at Progreso is lined with seafood restaurants, some with tables on the beach. For cheaper restaurants, head for the centre of town, near the bus terminal.

$$ Flamingo's
Calle 69 No 144-D and Calle 72.
Overlooking the ocean, **Flamingo's** serves wholesome fresh seafood, including fillets and coconut shrimp, standard Yucatec fare and good hot sauce. Strolling musicians may serenade you.

$$-$ Las Palmas and El Cocalito
2 of several reasonable fish restaurants in Chelem.

Bars and clubs

See also the free listings magazine *Yucatán Today*.

Cantina La Negrita
Calle 62 and 49 No 415.
Neighbourhood bohemian bar with lots of history, founded 1918. Buzzing, good crowd, fun vibe. Drinking up front, hearty food available out back. Modern and young, not a *cantina* in the traditional sense. Recommended.

Hennessy's Irish Pub
Paseo Montejo No 486-A, between 41 and 43.
Remarkably authentic Irish pub in a fantastic building on the Paseo Montejo, a social hub for the city's expatriates. Good cold beer, expensive food.

Mayan Pub
Calle 62, between Calles 55 and 57, www.mayanpub.com. Wed-Sun 0700-0300.
Superb outdoor colonial patio with ambient lighting, live music, jam sessions, Banksy wall art, beer, tequila, happy hours, snacks.

Entertainment

See the free listings magazine *Yucatán Today.*

Cinema
There is a cinema showing subtitled films in English on Parque Hidalgo. **Teatro Mérida**, Calle 62 between 59 and 61, shows European, Mexican and independent movies as well as live theatre productions. The 14-screen multiplex **Cinépolis** is in the huge Plaza de las Américas, north of the city; *colectivo* and buses take 20 mins and leave from Calle 65 between 58 and 60. For art house films, head to the intimate **Cairo Cinema Café**, Calle 20 No. 98A between Calles 15 and 17, Col Itzimná (take a taxi), www.cairocinemacafe.com.

Theatre
Teatro Peón Contreras
Calle 60 with 57.
One of the most beautiful theatres in Mexico, showing plays, ballet and orchestral performances. Shows start at 2100. For the latest programme, see www.merida.gob.mx/cultura.

Festivals

The city lays on a weekly programme of free cultural events. On Mon at 2100, there is a *vaquería*, with traditional Yucatec dancing, outside the Palacio Municipal; Tue at 2030, big band music in Parque de Santiago; Wed at 2100, a concert in the Centro Cultural Olimpio; Thu at 2100, Yucatec music, dance and song in the Parque Santa Lucía; Fri, usually an event in the University building, but not always; Sat at 2100, the 'Heart of Mérida' festival on the plaza and Calle 60; Sun, the central streets are closed to traffic, the plaza comes alive with music, performances and stalls.

6 Jan Mérida celebrates its birthday.
Feb/Mar Carnival takes place the week before Ash Wed (best on Sat). Floats, dancers in regional costume, music and dancing around the plaza and children dressed in animal suits.

Shopping

Crafts and souvenirs
You'll find an abundance of craft shops in the streets around the plaza. They sell hammocks (see box, page 31), silver jewellery, Panama hats, *guayabera* shirts, *huaraches*, baskets and Mayan figurines. The salesmen are ruthless, but they expect to receive about half their original asking price. Bargain hard, but maintain good humour, patience and face. And watch out for the many touts around the plaza, using all sorts of ingenious ploys to get you to their shops (and away from their competitors).

There are 2 main craft markets in the city: the **Mercado Municipal**, Calle 56a and 67 and the **García Rejón Bazaar**, Calle 65 and 60. The former sprawls, smells and takes over several blocks, but it's undeniably alive and undeniably Mexican. It sells everything under the sun and is also good for a cheap, tasty meal, but check the stalls for cleanliness. The latter is excellent for handicrafts and renowned for clothing, particularly leather *huaraches* and good-value cowboy boots – good, cheap Yucatecan fare. The state-sponsored **Casa de las Artesanías**, www.artesanias.yucatan.gob.mx, has several branches around the Yucatán, including **Tienda Matriz**, Calle 63 between Calle 64 and 66, and **Tienda Montejo**, Av Paseo de Montejo, opposite the Palacio Cantón; they sell everything from hammocks to *huipiles*, all made in the Yucatán, and provide social and economic programmes to support local artistic talent. For something special, **Artesanaria**, Calle 60 No 480 and Calle 55, deals in high-quality work.

If you're looking for a hammock, several places are recommended, but shop around for the best deal (also see box, page 31). **El Mayab**, Calle 58 No 553 and 71, are friendly, have a limited choice but good deals available; **La Poblana**, Calle 65 between Calle 58 and 60, will bargain, especially for sales of more than 1 – they have a huge stock. **El Aguacate**, Calle 58 No 604, corner of Calle 73, good hammocks and no hard sell. Recommended. **Casa de Artesanías Ki-Huic**, Calle 63, between Calle 62 and 64, is a friendly store with all sorts of handicrafts from silver and wooden masks, to hammocks and batik. Shop owner Julio Chay is very knowledgeable and friendly, sometimes organizes trips for visitors to his village, **Tixkokob**, which specializes in hammocks. Open daily, 0900-2100. Julio can also organize trips to other nearby villages and the shop has tequilas for sampling.

For silver, there are a handful of stores on Calle 60, just north of the plaza.

Mexican folk art, including *calaveras* (Day of the Dead skeletons), is available from **Minaturas**, Calle 59 No 507A; and **Yalat**, Calle 39 and 40.

If you're in the market for a *guayabera* shirt, you'll find stores all over the city, particularly on Calle 62, between 57 and 61.

What to do

Tour operators
Most tour operators can arrange trips to popular local destinations including Chichén Itzá, Uxmal, Celestún and nearby *cenotes*.
Carmen Travel Services, *Calle 27 No 151, between 32 and 34, T999-927 2027, www.carmentravel.com*. 3 other branches. This well-established agency can organize flights, hotels and all the usual trips to the sights. Recommended.
Ecoturismo Yucatán, *Calle 3 No 235, between Calle 32A and 34, T999-920 2772, www.ecoyuc.com.mx*. Specializes in educational and ecotourism tours including jungle trips, birding expeditions and turtle-hatching tours.

Language schools

Centro de Idiomas del Sureste, Calle 52 No 455, between 49 and 51, T999-923 0954, www.cisyucatan.com.mx. A well-established Spanish school offering tried and tested language and cultural programmes.
Modern Spanish Institute, Calle 15, No 500B, between 16A and 18, T999-911 0790, www.modernspanish.com. Courses in Spanish, Mayan culture, homestays.

Also offers adventure and archaeological packages.

Mayan Ecotours, *Calle 51 No 488 between Calles 54 and 56, T999-987 3710, www.mayanecotours.com*. An adventure and ecotourism operator offering high-quality tailor-made tours focussed on a variety of adrenaline-charged activities including rappelling, kayaking and mountain biking. They also offer trips to haciendas, archaeological sites and little-known *cenotes*.

Transport

Air

The airport is 8 km from the city. Bus 79 takes you to the centre; taxis to the centre charge US$12.

From Calle 67, 69 and 60, bus 79 goes to the airport, **Aeropuerto Rejón (MID)**, T999-946 1530, marked 'Aviación', US$0.50, roughly every 20 mins. Taxi set price voucher system US$8; *colectivo* US$2.50. Good domestic flight connections. International flight connections with **Belize City**, **Houston**, **Miami**, **San José** (Costa Rica), **Orlando** and **Havana**. Package tours Mérida–Havana–Mérida available (be sure to have a confirmed return flight). For return to Mexico ask for details at Secretaría de Migración Av Colón and Calle 8.

Bus

All buses from outside Yucatán State arrive at the **CAME** terminal on Calle 70 between Calle 69 and 71, several blocks south of the centre. There is a 2nd-class bus terminal, **TAME**, around the corner on Calle 69, where buses from local destinations such as Uxmal arrive.

There are several bus terminals in Mérida, as well as various *combis* for some local destinations (often more rapid).

The 1st-class bus station, **Terminal CAME**, Calle 70, between Calles 69 and 71, serves major destinations in Mexico and Yucatán State. Bus companies include **ADO**, **ADO GL**, **UNO**, **Platino** and **OCC**. The station has lockers and is open 24 hrs; left luggage charges from around US$0.50 per bag, depending on size. The walk to the centre is about 20 mins, taxi US$2.50. Schedules change frequently.

To **Cancún**, hourly, 4 hrs, US$24. To **Campeche**, hourly, 2 hrs, US$14. To **Chichén Itzá** (ruins and Pisté), 0630, 0915, 1240, 2 hrs, US$9; more frequent services from the 2nd-class Terminal TAME. To **Palenque**, 0830, 1915, 2200, 2300, 8 hrs, US$37. To **Tulum**, 1040, 1240, 1740, 2340, 4-5 hrs, US$20. To **Valladolid**, every 1-2 hrs, 1½ hrs, US$13. To **Villahermosa**, every 1-2 hrs, 9 hrs, US$43; and several **ADO GL** services, US$52. To **Tuxtla Guitérrez**, 5 daily with **OCC** and **ADO GL**, US$57-79. To **San Cristóbal de las Casas**, 1 daily with **OCC**, 1915, 15-16 hrs, US$52.

There are also 1st-class departures from the Hotel Fiesta Americana, Calle 60 and Colón, which are mostly 'luxury' services to **Cancún**.

Around the corner from CAME, the main 2nd-class bus station, **Terminal TAME**, Calle 69 between Calles 68 and 70, mostly serves destinations in the Yucatán Peninsula, including Uxmal, Chichén Itzá and the Ruta Puuc. Bus companies include **OCC**, **Mayab**, **Sur**, **FTS**, **Oriente** and **TRT**.

To **Cancún**, frequent departures, 5 hrs, US$15. To **Chichén Itzá**, hourly, 2-3 hrs, US$5.50. To **Ruta Puuc**, 2nd-class ATS service, Sun 0800, US$14. To **Uxmal**, 2nd-class **SUR** services at 0600, 0905, 1040, 1205, 1705, 1½ hrs, US$3.50. To **Valladolid**, hourly, 2 hrs, US$7.50

There is another 2nd-class terminal, **Terminal del Noreste**, near the market at Calle 50 and 65. It deals with obscure local destinations, including villages on the convent route, 11 departures daily, including **Acanceh**, **Tekit**, **Tecoh**, **Mamá**, **Chumayel**, **Teabo**, **Tipikal**, **Mani** and **Oxkutzcab**, US$1.25-3.60. To **Celestún**, frequent 2nd-class **Oriente** services, 2 hrs, US$3.50.

Buses to **Progreso** depart every 15 mins, US$1.25, from their own **Autoprogreso** terminal at Calle 62 No 524, between 65 and 67. For **Izamal**, it is fastest to use the *combis* that depart from Calles 65 and 54, 1 hr, US$3.50.

To Guatemala Take a bus from Mérida to San Cristóbal and change there for Comitán, or to Tenosique for the route to **Flores**. Another alternative would be to take the bus from Mérida direct to Tuxtla Gutiérrez (times given above), then connect to Ciudad Cuauhtémoc or to Tapachula.

To Belize Take a bus to **Chetumal**, **ADO** services at 0730 (except Wed and Sat), 1300, 1800, 2300, 6 hrs, US$30.50 and cross the border.

Car
Car hire Car reservations should be booked well in advance if possible. Hire firms charge around US$45-50 a day although bargains can be found in low season. All agencies allow vehicles to be returned to Cancún for an extra charge, and most have an office at the airport where they share the same counter and negotiating usually takes place. Agencies include: **Budget**, at the airport, T999-946 0762; **Easy Way Car Rental**, Calle 60, between 55 and 57, T999-930 9021, www.easywayrentacar-yucatan. com; **Mexico Rent a Car**, Calle 57A Depto 12, between 58 and 60, T999-923 3637, mexicorentacar@hotmail.com.

Taxi
Both fixed-priced and metered taxis are available. Metered taxis are identified by a 'Taximetro' sign on the roof; if using an unmetered taxi, always arrange the price beforehand. Most fares start at US$3.

There are various *sitio* stands, including **Sitio Santa Ana**, Calle 47 between Calle 58 and 60, T999-928 5000, www.taxiyturismo.com. Sample fares from downtown to Terminal CAME, US$4; to Gran Museo del Mundo Maya, US$5.50; to airport, US$11.50, to Hacienda Xcanatún, US$11.50; to Dzibilchaltún, US$15.

Celestún
Bus
Buses leave every 1-2 hrs from the local bus station on Calle 65 between 50 and 52, in **Mérida**, 2-hr journey, 2nd class US$3.50.

Progreso and around
Boat
Boats can be hired to visit the reef of **Los Alacranes** where many ancient wrecks are visible in clear water.

Bus
Buses from **Mérida** leave from the terminal on Calle 62 between 67 and 65, next to Hotel La Paz, every 10 mins. US$1.25. Returns every 10 mins until 2200.

Dzibilchaltún
Bus
5 direct buses a day on weekdays, from Parque San Juan, marked 'Tour/Ruta Polígono'; returns from the site entrance on the hour, passing the junction 15 mins later, taking 45 mins from the junction to **Mérida** (US$1).

Shuttles Leave from Parque San Juan in Mérida, corner of Calle 62 y 67A, every 1 or 2 hrs between 0500 and 1900.

The Convent Route
Mayan villages and ruins, colonial churches, cathedrals, convents and cenotes

For this route it's best to be on the road by 0800 with a full fuel tank. It's possible to explore the route using public transport (departures from the Noreste terminal on Calle 50), but keep an eye on the clock (few or no buses after dark) and consider overnighting in Ticul or Oxkutzcab. If driving, get on the Periférico to Ruta 18 (signs say Kanasín, not Ruta 18).

At **Kanasín**, La Susana is known especially for local delicacies like *sopa de lima*, *salbutes* and *panuchos*; it's clean, and there is excellent service and abundant helpings at reasonable prices. Follow the signs to **Acanceh**. Here you will see the unusual combination of the Grand Pyramid, a colonial church and a modern church, all on the same small plaza (similar to the Plaza de las Tres Culturas in Tlatelolco, Mexico City). About four blocks away is the Temple of the Stuccoes, with hieroglyphs. Eight kilometres further south is **Tecoh**, with an ornate church and convent dedicated to the Virgin of the Assumption. There are some impressive carved stones around the altar. The church and convent both stand at the base of a large Mayan pyramid. Nearby are the caverns of **Dzab-Náh**; you must take a guide as there are treacherous drops into *cenotes*. Next on the route is **Telchaquillo**, a small village with an austere chapel and a beautiful *cenote* in the plaza, with carved steps for easy access.

Mayapán and around
US$2.70.

A few kilometres off the main road to the right (west) you will find the Mayan ruins of **Mayapán**, a walled city with 4000 mounds, six of which are in varying stages of restoration. Mayapán, along with Uxmal and Chichén Itzá, once formed a triple alliance, and the site is as big as Chichén Itzá, with some buildings being replicas of those at the latter site. The restoration process is ongoing; the archaeologists can be watched as they unearth more and more buildings of this large, peaceful, late-Maya site. Mayapán is easily visited by bus from Mérida (every 30 minutes from terminal at Calle 50 y 67 behind the municipal market, one hour, US$1 to Telchaquillo). It can also be reached from Oxcutzcab.

Some 30 km along the main road is **Tekit**, a large village containing the church of San Antonio de Padua, with many ornate statues of saints. The next village, 7 km further on, is called **Mama**, with the oldest church on the route, famous for its ornate altar and bell-domed roof. Another 9 km is **Chumayel**, where the legendary Mayan document *Chilam Balam* was found. Four kilometres ahead is **Teabo**, with an impressive 17th-century church. Next comes **Tipikal**, a small village with an austere church.

Maní
Twelve kilometres further on is **Maní**, the most important stop on this route. Here you will find a large church, convent and museum with explanations in English,

Spanish and one of the Mayan languages. It was here that Fray Diego de Landa ordered important Mayan documents and artefacts to be burned, during an intense period of Franciscan conversion of the Maya people to Christianity. When Diego realized his great error, he set about trying to write down all he could remember of the 27 scrolls and hieroglyphs he had destroyed, along with 5000 idols, 13 altars and 127 vases. The text, entitled *Relation of Things in Yucatán*, is still available today, unlike the artefacts. To return to Mérida, head for Ticul, to the west, then follow the main road via Muná.

Ticul and Oxkutzcab

Eighty kilometres south of Mérida, **Ticul** is a small, pleasant little village known for its *huipiles*, the embroidered white dresses worn by the older Maya women. You can buy them in the tourist shops in Mérida, but the prices and quality of the ones in Ticul will be much better. It is also a good base for visiting smaller sites in the south of Yucatán State, such as Sayil, Kabah, Xlapak and Labná (see page 92).

Sixteen kilometres southeast of Ticul is **Oxkutzcab**, a good centre for catching buses to Chetumal, Muná, Mayapán and Mérida. It's a friendly place with a market by the plaza and a church with a 'two-dimensional' façade on the other side of the square.

Grutas de Loltún and around

Tue-Sun 0930, 1100, 1230 and 1400. US$8 Guided tours are at 0930, 1100, 1230, 1400, 1500, 1600; please tip generously.

Nearby, to the south, are the caverns and pre-Columbian vestiges at Loltún (supposedly extending for 8 km). Take a pickup (US$0.30) or truck from the market going to Cooperativa (an agricultural town). For return, flag down a passing truck. Alternatively, take a taxi, US$10 (can be visited from Labná on a tour from Mérida). The area around Ticul and Oxkutzcab is intensively farmed with citrus fruits, papayas and mangoes. After Oxkutzcab on Route 184 is **Tekax** with restaurant La Ermita serving excellent Yucatecan dishes at reasonable prices. From Tekax a paved road leads to the ruins of **Chacmultún**. From the top you have a beautiful view. There is a caretaker. All the towns between Muná and Peto, 14 km northeast of Oxkutzcab off Route 184, have large old churches. Beyond the Peto turn-off the scenery is scrub and swamp as far as the Belizean border.

Listings The Convent Route

Where to stay

Ticul

$$-$ Posada El Jardín
Calle 27 No 216c, between
Calles 28 and 30, T997-972 0401,
www.posadajardin.com.
Sweet little guesthouse with a handful of simple, economical, brightly painted rooms, a verdant garden, relaxing patios and a pool. Charming hosts.

Oxkutzcab

$$-$ Hotel Puuc
*Calle 55 No 80 and Calle 40, 997-975 0103
www.hotelpuuc.com.mx.*
Convenient, functional and modest motel-style lodgings, but very clean and comfortable. There's a splendid pool, a restaurant and parking. Rooms are cheaper without a/c.

Restaurants

Ticul

$$$-$$ Tutul-Xiu
Calle 29 No 191, between Calles 20 and 22.
Good-quality Yucatec and Mexican cuisine, including *poc chuc*, *queso relleno* and a host of turkey dishes, served by waitresses in traditional Yucatec dress. Also branches in Oxkutzcab, Maní and Mérida.

$$ Pizzería La Góndola
Calle 23, Ticul.
Good, moderately priced pizzas.

Transport

Ticul and Oxkutzcab
Colectivo
There are frequent VW *colectivos* to Ticul from Parque San Juan, **Mérida**, US$3.

The Puuc Route

hilly Mayan route south of Mérida

Taking in the four sites of Kabah, Sayil, Xlapak and Labná, as well as Uxmal, this journey explores the hilly (or *puuc* in Maya) region to the south of Mérida. All five sites can be visited in a day on the 'Ruta Puuc' bus, which departs from the first-class bus station in Mérida on Sunday at 0800, US$14, entry to sites not included, returns from Uxmal to Mérida at 1500. This is a good whistle-stop tour, but does not give you much time at each of the ruins, although five sites in one day is normally enough for most enthusiasts; if you want to spend longer seeing these sites, stay overnight in Ticul.

Kabah
0800-1700, US$3.25.

On either side of the main road, 37 km south of Uxmal and often included in tours of the latter, are the ruins of Kabah. On one side there is a fascinating **Palace of Masks** (*Codz-Poop*), whose façade bears the image of Chac, mesmerically repeated 260 times, the number of days in the Almanac Year. Each mask is made up of 30 units of mosaic stone. Even the central chamber is entered via a huge Chac mask whose curling snout forms the doorstep. On the other side of this wall, beneath the figure of the ruler, Kabal, are impressive carvings on the door arches, which depict a man about to be killed, pleading for mercy, and two men duelling. This side of the road is mostly reconstructed; across the road the outstanding feature is a reconstructed arch marking the start of the *sacbé* (sacred road), which leads all the way to Uxmal, and several stabilized but impossible to climb mounds of collapsed buildings being renovated. The style is Classic Puuc.

Sayil, Xlapak and Labná
Entrance US$3.25 at each site.

Sayil means 'The Place of the Ants'. Dating from AD 800-1000, this site has an interesting palace, which in its day included 90 bathrooms for some 350 people. The simple, elegant colonnade is reminiscent of the architecture of ancient Greece. The central motif on the upper part of the façade is a broad mask with huge fangs, flanked by two serpents surrounding the grotesque figure of a descending deity. From the upper level of the palace you can see a tiny ruin on the side of a mountain called the Nine Masks.

Some 13 km from Sayil, the ruins of **Xlapak** have not been as extensively restored as the others in this region. There are 14 mounds and three partially restored pyramids.

Labná has a feature that ranks it among the most outstanding sites of the Puuc region: a monumental arch connecting two groups of buildings (now in ruins), which displays an architectural concept unique to this region. Most Mayan arches are purely structural, but the one at Labná has been constructed for aesthetic purposes, running right through the façade and clearly meant to be seen from afar. The two façades on either side of the arch differ greatly; the one at the entrance is beautifully decorated with delicate latticework and stone carving imitating the wood or palm-frond roofs of Mayan huts.

Uxmal
Daily 0800-1700, US$14 including light and sound show; rental of translation equipment US$3. Shows are at 2000 in summer and 1900 in winter. Mixed reports. Guides available with 1½-hr tours. Tours in Spanish US$40, in English, French, German and Italian US$45. See Transport, below.

Built during the Classic period, Uxmal is the most famous of the ruins in the Puuc region. The characteristic features of Mayan cities in this region are the quadrangular layout of the buildings, set on raised platforms, and an artificially created underground water-storage system. The **Pyramid of the Sorcerer** is an unusual oval-shaped pyramid set on a large rectangular base; there is evidence that five stages of building were used in its construction. The pyramid is 30 m tall, with two temples at the top. The **Nunnery** is set around a large courtyard, with some fine masks of Chac, the rain god, on the corners of the buildings. The east building of the Nunnery is decorated with double-headed serpents on its cornices. There are some plumed serpents in relief, in excellent condition, on the façade of the west building.

The **House of the Governor** is 100 m long, and is considered one of the most outstanding buildings in all of Mesoamerica. Two arched passages divide the building into three distinct sections that would probably have been covered over. Above the central entrance is an elaborate trapezoidal motif, with a string of Chaac masks interwoven into a flowing, undulating serpent-like shape extending to the façade's two corners. The stately two-headed jaguar throne in front of the structure suggests a royal or administrative function.

The **House of the Turtles** is sober by comparison, its simple walls adorned with carved turtles on the upper cornice, above a short row of tightly packed columns, which resemble the Mayan *palapas*, made of sticks with a thatched roof, still used today. The **House of the Doves** is the oldest and most damaged of the buildings at Uxmal. It is still impressive: a long, low platform of wide columns topped by clusters of roof combs, whose similarity to dovecotes gave the building its name.

Listings The Puuc Route

Where to stay

Uxmal

There is no village at Uxmal, just some high-end hotels. For cheap accommodation, go to Ticul, 28 km away (see above) or to Santa Elena, 10 mins from the ruins by car.

$$$$ The Lodge at Uxmal
30 m from the entrance to ruins, T997-976 2102, www.mayaland.com/lodgeuxmal.
Luxurious Mayan-style *casitas* with tasteful wood furniture. Facilities include pool, restaurants, and spa. The same owners operate the comfortable **Hacienda Uxmal** (**$$$**), 400 m from the ruins (see website for more).

$$$-$$ The Fly-catcher Inn
Near the corner of Highway 261 and Calle 20, Santa Elena, T997-978 5350, www.flycatcherinn.com.
Pleasant B&B with verdant grounds and clean, comfortable rooms and *casitas* with a/c and screened windows. Prices include full breakfast.

$$ The Pickled Onion B&B
Highway 261 Uxmal–Kabah, Santa Elena, T997-111 7922, www.thepickledonionyucatan.com.
Friendly and helpful B&B with quaint Mayan-style accommodation, leafy garden and a pool. Rooms are simple, clean, comfortable and pleasant. Reiki and massage are available, there's Wi-Fi in public areas and a continental breakfast is included.

$$-$ Sacbé Bungalows
Highway 261 Km 159, Santa Elena, T997-978 5158, www.sacbebungalows.com.mx.
Set in 3 ha of verdant grounds, **Sacbé Bungalows** offers 8 simple, comfortable, clean, quiet and shaded bungalows. There's Wi-Fi and a pool.

Transport

Uxmal
Bus
5 buses a day from **Mérida**, from the terminal on Calle 69 between Calle 68 and 70, US$4. Return buses run every 2 hrs, or go to the entrance to the site on the main road and wait for a *colectivo*, which will take you to **Muná** for US$0.50. From there, many buses (US$1.70) and *colectivos* (US$1.40) go to Mérida.

Car
Parking at the site costs US$1 for the whole day. Uxmal is 74 km from **Mérida**,

177 km from **Campeche**, by a good paved road. If going by car from Mérida, there is a circular road round the city: follow the signs to Campeche, then 'Campeche via ruinas', then to 'Muná via Yaxcopoil' (long stretch of road with no signposting). Muná–Yaxcopoil is about 34 km. Parking US$1.

Izamal and around

friendly little town

Some 68 km east of Mérida is Izamal. Once a major Classic Maya religious site founded by the priest Itzamná, Izamal became one of the centres of the Spanish attempt to convert the Maya to Christianity.

Fray Diego de Landa, the historian of the Spanish conquest of Mérida (of whom there is a statue in the town), founded the huge **convent** and **church**, which now face the main **Plaza de la Constitución**. This building, constructed on top of a Mayan pyramid, was begun in 1549 and has the second largest atrium in the world. If you carefully examine the walls that surround the magnificent atrium, you will notice that some of the faced stones are embellished with carvings of Mayan origin, confirming that, when they had toppled the pre-Columbian structures, the Spaniards re-used the material to create the imported architecture. There is also a throne built for the Pope's visit in 1993. The image of the Inmaculada Virgen de la Concepción in the magnificent church was made the Reina de Yucatán in 1949, and the patron saint of the state in 1970.

Just 2½ blocks away, visible from the convent across a second square and signposted, are the ruins of a great mausoleum known as the **Kinich-Kakmo pyramid** ⓘ *0800-1700, free, entrance next to the tortilla factory.* You climb the first set of stairs to a broad, tree-covered platform, at the end of which is a further pyramid (still under reconstruction). From the top there is an excellent view of the town and surrounding henequen and citrus plantations. Kinich-Kakmo is 195 m long, 173 m wide and 36 m high, the fifth highest in Mexico.

In all, 20 Mayan structures have been identified in Izamal, several on Calle 27. Another startling feature about the town is that the entire colonial centre, including the convent, the arcaded government offices on Plaza de la Constitución and the arcaded second square, is painted a rich yellow ochre, giving it the nickname of the 'golden city'.

From Izamal you can go by bus to **Cenotillo**, where there are several fine *cenotes* within easy walking distance from the town (avoid the one in town), especially **Ucil**, excellent for swimming, and **La Unión**. Take the same bus as for Izamal from Mérida. Past Cenotillo is Espita and then a road forks left to Tizimín (see page 102).

The cemetery of **Hoctún**, on the Mérida–Chichén road, is also worth visiting; indeed it is impossible to miss, there is an 'Empire State Building' on the site. Take a bus from Mérida (last bus back 1700) to see extensive ruins at **Aké**, an unusual structure. Public transport in Mérida is difficult: from an unsigned stop on the corner of Calle 53 y 50, some buses to Tixkokob and Ekmul continue to Aké; ask the driver.

Listings Izamal

Where to stay

$$ Macan Ché
Calle 22 No 305 between Calle 33 and 35, T988-954 0287, www.macanche.com.
Intimate and friendly B&B with a lush tropical garden, pool, restaurant and hammocks. Comfortable rooms and *casitas*, all uniquely decorated. Recommended.

Restaurants

There are several restaurants on Plaza de la Constitución.

$$$-$$ Kinich
Calle 27 No 299 between Calle 28 and 30, www.kinichizamal.com.
Very good Mexican and Yucatec cuisine served in an open-air colonial courtyard. Rustic ambience and good service. It's located near the ruins of the same name.

$$-$ Los Arcos
Calle 28, between Calles 31 and 34, opposite Parque Zamná.
Simple and reasonably priced little eatery on the plaza serving wholesome tacos, quesadillas and other Mexican fare. Wi-Fi, breakfast and coffee too.

Shopping

Hecho a mano, *Calle 31A No 308 between 36 and 38.* A fine collection of Mexican folk art, postcards, textiles, jewellery, papier-mâché masks.
Market, *Calle 31, on Plaza de la Constitución, opposite convent.* Closes soon after lunch.

Transport

Bus
Bus station is on Calle 32 behind government offices, can leave bags, but better to take the *combi*, every 30 mins, US$4. 2nd class to **Mérida**, every 45 mins, 1½ hrs, US$1.50, lovely countryside. 6 a day to/from **Valladolid** (96 km), about 2 hrs, US$2.30-3.

Chichén Itzá

one of the most spectacular Mayan sites

★Chichén Itzá means 'mouth of the well of the water-sorcerer'. The Castillo, a giant-stepped pyramid, overlooks the site, watched over by Chacmool, a Maya fertility god who reclines on a nearby structure. The city was built by the Maya in late Classic times (AD 600-900). By the end of the 10th century, the city was more or less abandoned. It was re-established in the 11th to 12th centuries, but much debate surrounds by whom. Whoever the people were, a comparison of some of the architecture with that of Tula, north of Mexico City, indicates they were heavily influenced by the Toltecs of Central Mexico.

The major buildings in the north half display a Toltec influence. Dominating them is **El Castillo** ⓘ *1100-1500, 1600-1700, closed if raining*, its top decorated by the symbol of Quetzalcoatl/Kukulcán, the plumed serpent god. The balustrade of the 91 stairs up each of the four sides is also decorated at its base by the head of a plumed, open-mouthed serpent. The interior ascent of 61 steep and narrow steps

Essential Chichén Itzá

Entry fees

US$14 including light and sound show, free bag storage, free for Mexicans on Sun and holidays, when it is incredibly crowded; you may leave and reenter as often as you like on day of issue.

Tours

Guided tours US$40 per group of any size; it is best to try and join one, many languages available.

Opening hours

Daily 0800-1730. It's best to arrive before 1030 to beat the crowds.

Facilities

The tourist centre at the entrance to the ruins has a restaurant and small museum, bookshop and souvenir shop with exchange facilities. Drinks, snacks and toilets are available at the entrance and at the *cenote*.

What to take

Take a hat, suncream, sunglasses, shoes with good grip and drinking water.

> **Tip...**
> On the morning and afternoon of the spring and autumn equinoxes, the alignment of the sun's shadow casts a serpentine image on the side of the steps of El Castillo.

leading to a chamber is currently closed; the red-painted jaguar that probably served as the throne of the high priest once burned bright, its eyes of jade, its fangs of flint.

There is a **ball court** with grandstand and towering walls, each set with a projecting ring of stone high up; at eye-level is a relief showing the decapitation of the winning captain (sacrifice was an honour; some theories, however, maintain that it was the losing captain who was killed). El Castillo stands at the centre of the northern half of the site, and almost at a right angle to its northern face runs the *sacbé* (sacred road), to the **Cenote Sagrado** (Well of Sacrifice). Into the Cenote Sagrado were thrown valuable propitiatory objects of all kinds, animals and human sacrifices. The well was first dredged by Edward H Thompson, the US Consul in Mérida, between 1904 and 1907; he accumulated a vast quantity of objects in pottery, jade, copper and gold. In 1962 the well was explored again by an expedition sponsored by the National Geographic Society and some 4000 further artefacts were recovered, including beads, polished jade, lumps of *copal* resin, small bells, a statuette of rubber latex, another of wood, and a quantity of animal and human bones. Another *cenote*, the Cenote Xtoloc, was probably used as a water supply. To the east of El Castillo is the **Templo de los Guerreros** (Temple of the Warriors) with its famous reclining **Chacmool** statue. This pyramidal platform is closed off to avoid erosion.

Chichén Viejo (Old Chichén), where the Mayan buildings of the earlier city are found, lies about 500 m by path from the main clearing. The famous **El Caracol**, or Observatory, is included in this group, as is the **Casa de las Monjas** (Nunnery). A

Chichén Itzá

Main Entrance

North Half

South Half

OLD CHICHEN

Entrance from Hotels

N

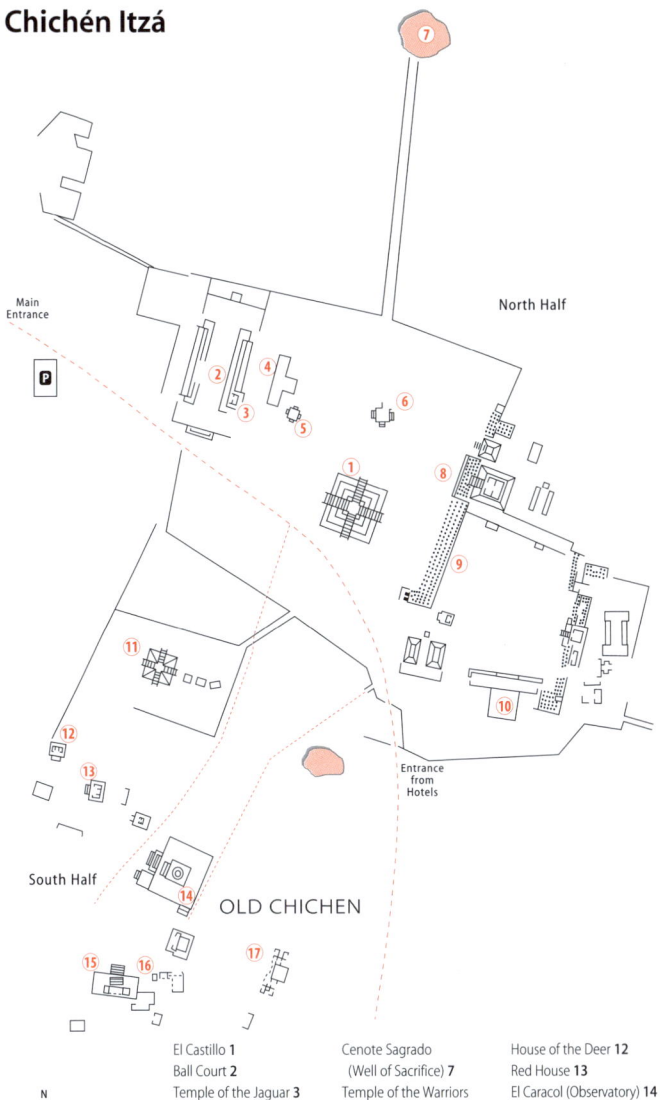

100 metres
100 yards

El Castillo **1**
Ball Court **2**
Temple of the Jaguar **3**
Platform of the Skulls (Tzompantli) **4**
Platform of Eagles **5**
Platform of Venus **6**
Cenote Sagrado (Well of Sacrifice) **7**
Temple of the Warriors & Chacmool Statue **8**
Group of a Thousand Columns **9**
Market **10**
Tomb of the High Priest **11**
House of the Deer **12**
Red House **13**
El Caracol (Observatory) **14**
Casa de las Monjas (Nunnery) **15**
'Church' **16**
Akabdzilo **17**

Cancún & Yucatán Peninsula Yucatán State • 97

footpath to the right of the Casa de las Monjas leads to the **Templo de los Tres Dinteles** (Temple of the Three Lintels) after 30 minutes' walking. It requires at least one day to see the many pyramids, temples, ball courts and palaces, all of them adorned with astonishing sculptures. Excavation and renovation is still going on. Interesting birdlife and iguanas can also be seen around the ruins.

Grutas de Balankanché

0900-1700, US$7.50 (allow about 45 mins for the 300-m descent), closed Sat afternoons. Guided tours in English at 1100, 1300, 1500; in Spanish at 0900, 1000, 1100, 1200, 1300.

Tours run daily to the Grutas de Balankanché caves, 3 km east of Chichén Itzá just off the highway. There are archaeological objects, including offerings of pots and *metates* in an extraordinary setting, except for the unavoidable, awful *son et lumière* show (five a day in Spanish; 1100, 1300 and 1500 in English; 1000 in French; it is very damp and hot, so dress accordingly). To get there, take the Chichén Itzá or Pisté-Balankanché bus hourly at a quarter past, US$0.50, taxi US$15.

Listings Chichén Itzá

Where to stay

$$$$ Hacienda Chichén
T999-924 8407,
www.haciendachichen.com.
Luxury resort and spa, close to the ruins, with tasteful rooms, suites and bungalows. There's a garden, library and restaurant, all contained in historic colonial grounds.

$$$-$$ Hotel Chichén Itzá
Pisté, T999-851 0022,
www.mayaland.com.
Large hotel with 3 types of rooms and tariffs. The best are clean, tasteful, overlook the garden and have a/c, internet, phone and fridge. Cheaper rooms overlook the street.

$$$-$$ Villas Arqueológicas
T997-974 6020, Carretera Mérida–Valladolid Km 120, Piste,
www.villasarqueologicas.com.mx, 800 m from the ruins.
A large hotel with a tropical garden, small pool, book collection, and 45 clean and comfortable rooms. The restaurant is on the expensive side, beds are quite firm, but otherwise a tranquil and pleasant lodging.

$$ Dolores Alba Chichén
Km 122, T985-858 1555,
www.doloresalba.com.
Small, Spanish-owned hotel, 2.5 km on the road to Puerto Juárez (bus passes it), 40 clean if old bungalows with shower, a/c and cable TV. Pool, restaurant, English is spoken, free morning shuttle to the ruins.

$$-$ Pirámide Inn Resort
1.5 km from ruins, at the Chichén end of Pisté, Km 117, T999-851 0115,
www.chichen.com.
Economical and functional Pisté option with many clean, colourful rooms, a pool, hammocks and *palapas*. *Temazcal* available, book 24 hrs in advance.

Camping costs US$5, or US$15 with a car. Friendly owner, speaks English.

Restaurants

Mostly poor and overpriced in Chichén itself (cafés inside the ruins are cheaper than the restaurant at the entrance, but still expensive). You can also try the larger hotels. Barbecued chicken is available on the streets of Pisté, sit-down restaurants close 2100-2200.

$$ Fiesta Maya
Calle 15 No 59, Pisté.
Reportedly the best restaurant in town. Serves Yucatecan food, tacos, meat and sandwiches. Lunch buffet every day at 1200, US$10.

$ Sayil
In Pisté.
Serves Yucatecan dishes like *pollo pibil*, as well as breakfast *huevos al gusto*.

Festivals

21 Mar and 21 Sep On the morning and afternoon of the spring and autumn equinoxes, the alignment of the sun's shadow casts a serpentine image on the side of the steps of El Castillo. This occasion is popular and you'll be lucky to get close enough to see the action. Note that this phenomenon can also be seen on the days before and after the equinox, 19th-23rd of the month.

Transport

ADO bus office in Pisté is between Stardust and Pirámide Inn. Budget travellers going on from Mérida to Isla Mujeres or Cozumel should visit Chichén from Valladolid (see below), although if you plan to go through in a day you can store luggage at the visitor centre.

Bus
Frequent 2nd-class buses depart from Mérida to Cancún, passing Chichén Itzá and Pisté. Likewise, there are frequent departures to/from Valladolid. To **Mérida**, 2nd class, hourly, US$5.50; and 1st class, 1420 and 1700, US$9. To **Cancún**, 2nd class, hourly, US$9. To **Valladolid**, 2nd class, hourly, US$2.50. To **Tulum**, 2nd class, 0810, 1420, 1615, US$11. The ruins are a 5-min ride from Pisté – the buses drop off and pick up passengers until 1700 at the top of the coach station opposite the entrance.

Valladolid and around

handsome colonial city unspoilt by tourism

Situated roughly halfway between Mérida and Cancún, Valladolid is filled with colourful houses, cobblestone streets, historic churches and plazas. There is a slightly medieval feel to the place, some of the streets tapering off into mud tracks. The *Vallisoletanos*, as they are known, are friendlier than their *Meridano* neighbours, and Valladolid's location makes it an ideal place to settle for a few days while exploring the ruins of Chichén Itzá, the fishing village of Río Lagartos, and the three beautiful *cenotes* in the area, one of which is right in the town itself. Valladolid is still relatively untouched by tourism (aside from the cavalcade of monstrous tour buses on the plaza every afternoon), but it is now showing signs of gentrification. The town is small and easily explored on foot.

Sights

Valladolid is set around a large plaza flanked by the imposing Franciscan **cathedral** (which is more impressive outside than in) and the **Palacio de Gobierno**, which has striking murals inside. Most of the hotels are clustered around the centre, as well as numerous restaurants catering for all budgets. Just off the plaza, **Casa de los Venados** ⓘ *Calle 40 No 204, T985-856-2289, www.casadelosvenados.com, guided*

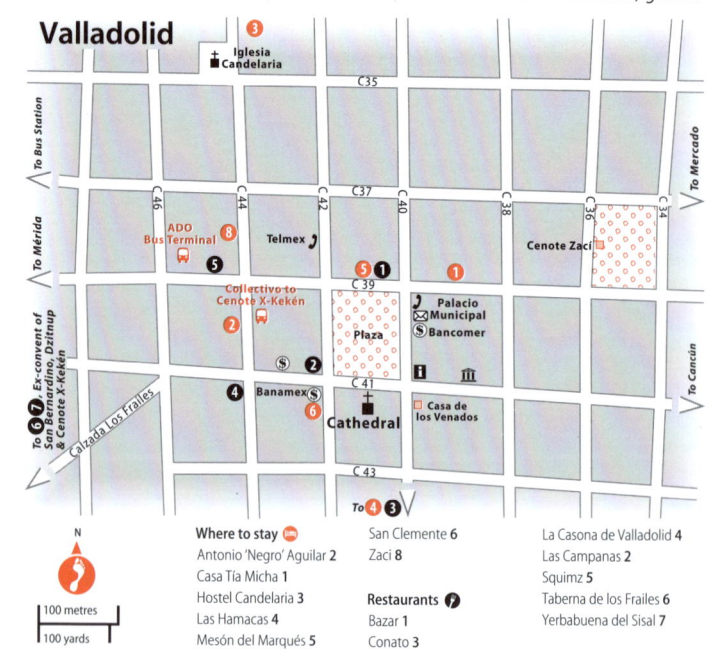

Where to stay
Antonio 'Negro' Aguilar 2
Casa Tía Micha 1
Hostel Candelaria 3
Las Hamacas 4
Mesón del Marqués 5
San Clemente 6
Zaci 8

Restaurants
Bazar 1
Conato 3
La Casona de Valladolid 4
Las Campanas 2
Squimz 5
Taberna de los Frailes 6
Yerbabuena del Sisal 7

100 • Cancún & Yucatán Peninsula Yucatán State

tours Mon-Fri 1000, suggested donation US$3, is a private home with a stunning collection of Mexican folk art, painstakingly acquired over a decade by enthusiasts John and Dorianne Venator.

The **Calzada de los Frailes** is a historic lane running diagonally southwest from the corner of Calles 46 and 41. Near its entrance, there is a tequila tour, **Los Tres Toños** ⓘ *Calle 41 No 222, 1000-2000*, where you can learn about production techniques and sample some local liquor; the tour is free, essentially a sales pitch for the distillery. Further down the Calzada is a little chocolate factory also offering 'free' tours with samples at the end. At the conclusion of the calzada, the 16th-century **Ex-Convento de San Bernardino** ⓘ *Mon-Sat, 0900-1800, US$2*, is one of Mexico's most important Franciscan structures, more of a fortress than a convent. It contains interesting frescoes and sacred art, as well as gardens pleasant for strolling.

Cenote Zací ⓘ *Calle 36 between Calle 37 and 39, daily 0800-1800, US$3, half price for children*, right in town, is an artificially lit *cenote* where you can swim, except when it is occasionally prohibited due to algae in the water. There is a thatched restaurant and lighted promenades. A small town **museum** ⓘ *Calle 41, free*, housed in Santa Ana church, shows the history of rural Yucatán and has some exhibits from recent excavations at the ruins of Ek-Balam.

★Cenote Dzitnup
Daily 0800-1800, US$2.50. Colectivos leave when full from in front of Hotel María Guadalupe, US$1, returning until 1800, after which you'll have to get a taxi back to Valladolid, US$6.

Seven kilometres from Valladolid is the beautiful **Cenote X-Kekén**, at **Dzitnup**, the name by which it is more commonly known. It is stunningly lit with electric lights, the only natural light source being a tiny hole in the cavernous ceiling dripping with stalactites. Swimming is excellent, the water is cool and refreshing, although reported to be a little dirty, and harmless bats zip around overhead. Exploratory walks can also be made through the many tunnels leading off the *cenote*, for which you will need a torch. There is also the easily reached *cenote* close by, called **Samulá** ⓘ *US$3*, only recently opened to the public.

Ek-Balam
Daily 0800-1700, US$7.50. To get there by car, take Route 295 north out of Valladolid. Just after the village of Temozón, turn right for Santa Rita. The ruins are 5 km further on. Colectivos to Ek Balam depart from Calle 44 between Calle 37 and 35, 4-person minimum, US$3. A round-trip taxi with a wait is around US$20.

Some 25 km north of Valladolid are the Mayan ruins of Ek-Balam, meaning 'Black Jaguar'. The ruins contain an impressive series of temples, sacrificial altars and residential buildings grouped around a large central plaza. The main temple, known as 'The Tower', is an immaculate seven-tiered staircase leading up to a flattened area with the remains of a temple. The views are stunning and, because they are not on the tourist trail, these ruins can be viewed at leisure, without the presence of hordes of tour groups from Cancún.

Río Lagartos and around

Tizimín is a dirty, scruffy little town en route to Río Lagartos, where you will have to change buses. If stuck, there are several cheap *posadas* and restaurants, but with frequent buses to Río Lagartos, there should be no need to stay the night here.

Río Lagartos is an attractive little fishing village on the north coast of Yucatán State, whose main attraction is the massive biosphere reserve containing thousands of pink flamingos, as well as 250 other species of bird. The people of Río Lagartos are extremely friendly and very welcoming to tourists. The only route is on the paved road from Valladolid; access from Cancún is by boat only, a journey mainly made by tradesmen ferrying fish to the resort. Development in Río Lagartos, however, is on the horizon.

Boat trips to see the flamingo reserve can be easily arranged by walking down to the harbour and taking your pick from the many offers you'll receive from boatmen. You will get a longer trip with fewer people, due to the decreased weight in the boat. As well as flamingos, there are 250 other species of bird, some very rare, in the 47-sq-km reserve. Make sure your boatman takes you to the larger colony of flamingos near **Las Coloradas** (15 km), recognizable by a large salt mound on the horizon, rather than the smaller groups of birds along the river. Early morning boat trips can be arranged in Río Lagartos to see the flamingos (US$40-55, in eight to nine seater, 2½ to four hours, cheaper in a five-seater, fix the price before embarking; in midweek few people go so there is no chance of negotiating, but boat owners are more flexible on where they go; at weekends it is very busy, so it may be easier to get a party together and reduce costs). Check before going whether the flamingos are there; they usually nest here during May and June and stay through July and August (although salt mining is disturbing their habitat).

Listings Valladolid and around *map p100*

Tourist information

Tourist office
Southeast corner of the plaza.
Maps, general information and flyers.

Where to stay

$$$ Casa Tía Micha
Calle 39 No 197, T985-856 0499, www. casatiamicha.wix.com/casatiamicha.
Boutique colonial-style hotel with 1 room and 2 suites, very intimate and romantic; 1 'luxury suite' with jacuzzi and wine, 1 'honeymoon suite' with 4-poster bed. Very helpful staff and hospitable hosts. Recommended.

$$$ Hotel Las Hamacas
Calle 49 No 202-A, T985-100 4270, www.casahamaca.com.
Denis Larsen has done an extraordinary and commendable job with his friendly and hospitable B&B, which is

set in verdant grounds, with a pool, 8 comfortable suites and an English-language library. It's adorned with indigenous art and artefacts; shamanic therapies are available. A storehouse of information on the area.

$$$ Mesón del Marqués
Calle 39 with Calle 40 and 42, north side of Plaza Principal, T985-856 2073, www.mesondelmarques.com.
Housed in a handsome colonial edifice, this hotel has 90 tasteful rooms, all with a/c and cable TV. There's a pool, Wi-Fi, garden and laundry service. Check the room before accepting. Recommended.

$$ Hotel Zaci
Calle 44 No 191, between Calles 37 and 39, T985-856 2167, www.hotel zaci.com.mx.
Large hotel with good-value rooms overlooking a narrow central courtyard, with a small pool, 48 standards, 12 premier, solid wood furniture, simple, comfortable.

$$ San Clemente
Calle 42 No 206, T985-856 2208, www.hotelsanclemente.com.mx.
Located right on the plaza, rooms are large, comfortable and overlook a central courtyard. They are cleaned daily, although some are a bit musty. It's good value and a great price for the location. There's also a pool and a café.

$ Antonio 'Negro' Aguilar
The rooms are on Calle 41 No 225, but you need to book them at Aguilar's shop (Calle 44 No 195, T985-856 2125. If the shop's closed, knock on the door of the house on the right of the shop).
Rents rooms for 2, 3 or 4 people. The best budget deal in the town for 2 or more, clean, spacious rooms on a quiet street, garden, volleyball/ basketball court.

$ Hostel Candelaria
Calle 35 No 201F, between Calles 42 and 44, Parque de Candelaria, T985-856 2267, www.hostel valladolidyucatan.com.
Fantastic location on the lovely Plaza Candelaria, townhouse with a great garden, benches, tree growing through the centre. Best hostel in town.

Río Lagartos and around

$$ Villa de Pescadores
Calle 14 No 93, on the malecón T986-862 0020, www.hotelriolagartos.com.mx.
The best option in town, functional, simple and clean. They have 11 rooms, some with balconies, breezes and expansive views over the harbour, worth the extra pesos.

Restaurants

$$$ Conato
Calle 40 No 226, between Calles 45 y 47.
Atmospheric bohemian bar-restaurant with Frida Kahlo artwork, antiques and vibrant Mexican folk art. They serve Mexican staples, hearty and reasonable international fare too. Kitsch place, mellow vibe.

$$$ La Casona de Valladolid
Calle 41 and 44, T985-100 7040.
People come for the lunch buffet ($$$), which includes Yucatec specialities. Good setting and atmosphere with a splendid colonial building and lots of folk art. Seating is on a large outdoor patio, many tables, frequent tour groups.

$$$ Taberna de los Frailes
Calle 49 No 235, www.tabernadelosfrailes.com.
Romantic setting near the Convent of San Bernardino, lots of character, fabulous building and garden. They serve

Yucatec and Mayan specialities, a bit pricey for the town, but very beautiful.

$$ Las Campanas
Calle 42, Parque Central.
Reasonable Mexican fare, some of it good. An atmospheric building and lots of diners in the evenings.

$$-$ Squimz
Calle 39 No 219, between Calles 44 and 46, www.squimz.com.mx.
Modern, airy café with casual booth seating up front and a relaxing patio out back. Good breakfasts, coffee, sandwiches and some international fare. Wi-Fi and attentive service.

$$-$ Yerbabuena del Sisal
Calle 54A No 217.
Lovely lunch café serving Yucatec treats and staple snacks made with healthy fresh ingredients, including revitalizing fruit and juices, spicy salsas, hot tortillas and salads prepared with love.

$ Bazar
Northeast corner of Plaza Principal, next to Mesón del Marqués.
Wholesome grub, a bit hit and miss, it's best to choose a popular kitchen and ignore the excitable waiters trying to lure you in.

Río Lagartos and around
For a fishing village, the seafood is not spectacular, as most of the good fish is sold to restaurants in Mérida and Cancún.

$$ Isla Contoy
Calle 19 No 134.
Average seafood, not cheap for the quality.

$$ Los Negritos
Off the plaza.
Moderately priced seafood.

Festivals

Río Lagartos and around
17 Jul A big local **fiesta**, with music, food and dancing in the plaza.
12 Dec **Virgen de Guadalupe**. The whole village converges on the chapel built in 1976 on the site of a vision of the Virgin Mary by a local non-believer, who suddenly died, along with his dog, shortly after receiving the vision.

Transport

Bus
The **ADO** bus terminal is on Calle 39 and 46, 2 blocks from the main plaza. To **Cancún**, ADO, frequent, 2½ hrs, US$12.50; and many 2nd class, 3-4 hrs, US$6. To **Chichén Itzá**, ADO, 4 daily, 30 mins; US$5.25; and many 2nd class, US$2.50. To **Mérida**, ADO, 16 daily, 2½ hrs, US$13. To **Playa del Carmen**, 6 daily, 3 hrs, US$12.50. To **Tizimín** (for Río Lagartos), frequent 1 hr, US$2. To **Tulum**, 4 daily, US$7.50.

Río Lagartos and around
Bus
There are 2 terminals side by side in Tizimín. If coming from Valladolid en route to Río Lagartos, you will need to walk to the other terminal. Tizimín–Río Lagartos, 7 per day, 1½ hrs, US$2. To **Valladolid**, frequent, 1 hr, US$2. To **Mérida**, several daily, 4 hrs, US$4. There are also buses to **Cancún**, **Felipe Carrillo Puerto** and **Chetumal**.

It is possible to get to Río Lagartos and back in a day from **Valladolid**, if you leave on the 0630 or 0730 bus (taxi Tizimín–Río Lagartos US$25, driver may negotiate). Last bus back from Río Lagartos at 1730.

Campeche State

The state of Campeche embraces the torpid Gulf coast of the Yucatán Peninsula. It enjoys a special prosperity thanks to its offshore oil reserves, exploited by Pemex since the 1970s. Despite its huge potential as a destination, next to the big tourist hubs of Quintana Roo and Yucatán states, relatively few travellers take the time to explore Campeche. But those who do invariably discover a land steeped in history and legends, as vivid and compelling as any of the Yucatán's hot spots.

The state capital, Campeche City, recalls the age of seafarers and pirates with its crumbling city walls and defensive forts, a bastion of colonial grandeur standing sentinel on the coast. Inland, the landscape alternates between savannah and rainforest, the setting for scores of distinctive Mayan ruins. The Chenes, Puuc and Río Bec architectural styles are all represented, triumphs of extraordinary aesthetic form, but nothing beats the mighty Calakmul for sheer size, its behemoth pyramids and temples testament to the vast power of the early Mayan city states. South of the capital, the sweltering Gulf coast is a lesser visited stretch of windswept beaches, sluggish mangroves, yawning estuaries and wildlife-rich lagoons, including Laguna de Términos.

For those willing to get off the beaten track, Campeche promises adventure and intrigue, blissfully free from crowds.

Campeche City

a laid-back, bohemian historic quarter and an appealing seafront promenade

Oil profits have gone a long way to revitalizing the economy of the ancient fortified city of Campeche: neatly hidden behind traffic-choked streets, its Centro Histórico has enjoyed an extensive programme of restoration since the 1980s. It is now rapidly becoming gentrified and has been a UNESCO World Heritage Site since 1999. Replete with cafés and art galleries, the area also has pretty pastel-shaded townhouses and cobblestone streets. Beyond the city walls, the seafront *malecón* is an extensive promenade where people stroll, cycle, walk and relax in the evening in the light of the setting sun.

Like many Yucatán towns, Campeche's streets in the Old Town are numbered rather than named. Even numbers run north–south beginning at Calle 8 (no one knows why) near the *malecón*, east to Calle 18 inside the walls; odd numbers run east (inland) from Calle 51 in the north to Calle 65 in the south. Most of the points of interest are within this compact area. Connecting sea and land gates, Calle 59 has now been pedestrianized with great success. A full circuit of the walls is a long walk; buses marked 'Circuito Baluartes' provide a regular service around the perimeter.

Sights

Of the original walls, seven of the *baluartes* and an ancient fort (now rather dwarfed by two big white hotels on the seafront) remain; some house museums (see below).

The heart of the city is the **Zócalo**, where the austere Franciscan **cathedral** (1540-1705) has an elaborately carved façade; inside is the Santo Entierro (Holy Burial), a sculpture of Christ on a mahogany sarcophagus with a silver trim. There is plenty of shade under the trees in the Zócalo and a small pagoda with a snack bar.

Right in front of the Zócalo is the **Baluarte de Nuestra Señora de la Soledad**, the central bulwark of the city walls, from where you can do a walking tour of the **Circuito Baluartes**, the remains of the city walls. Heading east, you will come to the **Puerta del Mar**, formerly the entrance for those permitted to enter the city from the sea, which used to come up to this point. Next along the *circuito* is a pair of modern buildings, the **Palacio de Gobierno** and the **Congreso**. The latter looks like a flying saucer and makes for a bizarre sight when viewed with the 17th-century **Baluarte de San Carlos** in the background. Baluarte de San Carlos now houses the **Museo de la Ciudad**. Heading west on the continuation of the *circuito*, you will come to **Templo de San José**, on Calle 10, an impressive baroque church with a beautifully tiled façade. It has been de-consecrated and is now an educational centre. Back on to the *circuito*, you will next reach the **Baluarte de Santa Rosa**, now the home of the tourist information office. Next is **Baluarte de San Juan**, from which a large chunk of the old city wall still extends, protecting you from the noisy traffic on the busy road beyond. The wall connects with **Puerta de la Tierra** ⓘ *Tue, Fri and Sat 2000 (for information, contact the tourist office), US$4*, where a *Luz y Sonido* (Light and Sound) show takes place. The continuation of the *circuito* will take you past the **Baluarte de San Francisco** and then past the market, just outside the line of the city walls. **Baluarte de San Pedro** flanks the northeast corner of the city centre and now houses a museum. The *circuito* runs down to the northwest tip of the old city, where the **Baluarte de Santiago** houses the Botanical Gardens.

There are a few cultural centres in Campeche. The **Casa del Teniente de Rey** ⓘ *Calle 59 No 38 between 14 and 16, T981-811 1314, www.inah.gob.mx*, houses the **Instituto Nacional de Antropología e Historia (INAH)**, dedicated to the restoration of Mayan ruins in the state of Campeche, as well as supporting local museums. INAH can be visited for information regarding any of the sites in the state. The **Centro Cultural Casa 6** ⓘ *Calle 57, between Calle 8 and 10, daily 0900-2100, US$0.35*, is housed in a handsome building on the main plaza. It conjures the opulence and splendour of Campeche's golden days.

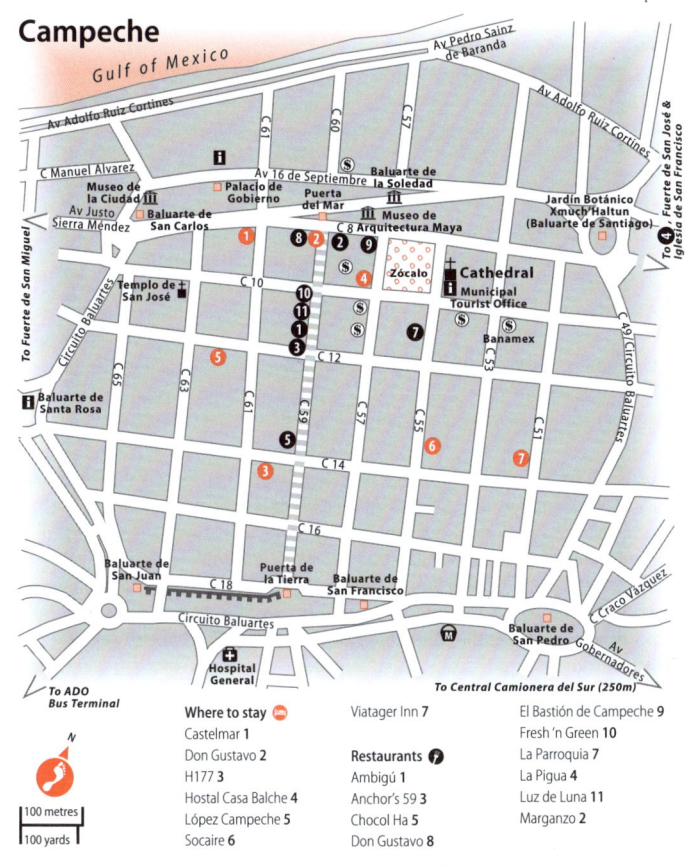

Campeche

Where to stay
Castelmar 1
Don Gustavo 2
H177 3
Hostal Casa Balche 4
López Campeche 5
Socaire 6
Viatager Inn 7

Restaurants
Ambigú 1
Anchor's 59 3
Chocol Ha 5
Don Gustavo 8
El Bastión de Campeche 9
Fresh 'n Green 10
La Parroquia 7
La Pigua 4
Luz de Luna 11
Marganzo 2

BACKGROUND
Campeche

Highway 180 enters the city as the Avenida Resurgimiento, passing either side of the huge **Monumento al Resurgimiento**, a stone torso holding aloft the Torch of Democracy. Originally the trading village of Ah Kim Pech, it was here that the Spaniards, under Francisco Hernández de Córdoba, first disembarked on Mexican soil (22 March 1517) to replenish their water supply. For fear of being attacked by the native population, they quickly left, only to be attacked later by the locals further south in Champotón, where they were forced to land by appalling weather conditions at sea. It was not until 1540 that Francisco de Montejo managed to conquer Ah Kim Pech, founding the city of Campeche on 4 October 1541, after failed attempts in 1527 and again in 1537.

The export of local dyewoods, *chicle*, timber and other valuable cargoes soon attracted the attention of most of the famous buccaneers, who constantly raided the port from their bases on Isla del Carmen, then known as the Isla de Tris. Combining their fleets for one momentous swoop, they fell upon Campeche on 9 February 1663, wiped out the city and slaughtered its inhabitants. Five years later the Crown began fortifying the site, the first Spanish colonial settlement to be completely walled. Formidable bulwarks, 3 m thick and 'a ship's height', and eight bastions (*baluartes*) were built in the next 36 years. All these fortifications soon put a stop to pirate attacks and Campeche prospered as one of only two Mexican ports (the other was Veracruz) to have had the privilege of conducting international trade.

After Mexican Independence from Spain, the city declined into an obscure fishing and logging town. Only with the arrival of a road from the 'mainland' in the 1950s and the oil boom of the 1970s has Campeche begun to see visitors in any numbers, attracted by its historical monuments and relaxed atmosphere (*campechano* has come to mean an easy-going, pleasant person).

Further from the city walls is the **Batería de San Luis**, 4 km south from the centre along the coast road. This was once a lookout post to catch pirates as they approached the city from a distance. The **Fuerte de San Miguel**, 600 m inland, is now a museum. A 20-minute walk along Avenida Miguel Alemán from Baluarte de Santiago is the 16th-century **San Francisco** church, with wooden altars painted in vermilion and white. Nearby is the **Portales de San Francisco**, a beautifully restored old entrance to the city, with several good restaurants in its shadow.

The **Museo de Arquitectura Maya** ⓘ *Baluarte de Nuestra Señora de la Soledad, Tue-Sun, 0800-1930, US$2.70*, has three well-laid-out rooms of Mayan stelae and sculpture. **Jardín Botánico Xmuch'Haltun** ⓘ *Baluarte de Santiago, Mon-Sat 0900-2100, Sun 0900-1600, US$0.80*, is a small but perfectly formed collection of tropical plants and flowers in a peaceful setting. The **Fuerte de San Miguel** ⓘ *Tue-Sun 0900-1930, US$2.50*, on the *malecón* 4 km southwest, is the most atmospheric of the forts (complete with drawbridge and a moat said to have once contained either crocodiles or skin-burning lime, take your pick!); it houses the **Museo de Cultura Maya** ⓘ *Tue-Sun 0900-1730*, with a well-documented display of pre-Columbian exhibits including jade masks and black funeral pottery from Calakmul and recent finds from Jaina.

Around Campeche

Lerma is virtually a small industrial suburb of Campeche, with large shipyards and fish-processing plants; the afternoon return of the shrimping fleet is a colourful sight. The **Fiesta de Polk Kekén** is held on 6 January, with traditional dances. The nearest decent beaches are at Seybaplaya (see page 115), 20 km south of Campeche. There, the beaches are clean and deserted; take your own food and drink as there are no facilities. Crowded, rickety buses marked 'Lerma' or 'Playa Bonita' run from Campeche, US$1.50, 8 km.

Listings Campeche City *map p107*

Tourist information

For a good orientation take the Centro Histórico tour, a regular tourist tram running daily from the main plaza on the hour 0900-1200 and 1700-2000, 45 mins, US$7.50, English and Spanish spoken.

Municipal tourist office
Calle 55 No 3, T019 816 3989, www.campeche.travel.
Located next to the cathedral and supplemented by an information booth on the plaza.

State tourist office
On the malecón. Av Ruiz Cortines s/n, T981-127 3300, www.campeche.travel. On the malecón.

Where to stay

$$$$ Don Gustavo
Calle 59 No 4, T01800-839 0959, www.casadongustavo.com.
Classic colonial beauty at this upmarket boutique hotel, a converted townhouse. Suites are simple and elegant, crisply attired and adorned with delicate antiques. Pleasant patios, spa facilities and a superb restaurant. The best in town.

$$$$ Hacienda Uayamon
Carretera Uayamon–China–Edzná Km 20, T981-813 0530, www. haciendauayamon.com.
This beautiful old hacienda has been tastefully restored to its former elegance and now serves as a luxury hotel. Rooms are handsome, combining traditional and contemporary flourishes. The grounds, setting and architecture are superb.

$$$ Castelmar
Calle 61, between Calle 8 and 10, T981-811 1204, www.castelmar hotel.com.
Fantastic early 19th-century building, a former military barracks, now one of the oldest hotels in town and decorated in grand colonial style. Its 26 rooms are smart, clean, spacious and decorated with solid wooden furniture and fine tiled floors.

$$$ Hotel Socaire
Calle 55 No 22, between Calles 12 and 14, T981-811 2130, www.hotelsocaire.com.mx.
A youthful new hotel with 8 good, clean, well-equipped rooms, simple, stylish and modern. There's also a decent restaurant attached, friendly staff and a small pool. Calm and welcoming colours. Recommended.

$$$-$$ Hotel H177
Calle 14 No 177, between Calles 59 and 61, T981-816 4463, www.h177hotel.com.mx.
A modern lodging with a trendy look. Brand new rooms include comfortable singles, doubles and suites, all crisply attired with white linen and red curtains. Facilities include spa and jacuzzi.

$$ Hotel López Campeche
Calle 12 No 189 between Calles 61 and 63, T981-816 3344, www.hotellopezcampeche.com.mx.
An interesting art deco building with 50 clean, simple, comfortable rooms overlooking an inner courtyard. Facilities include a small pool, café and all modern conveniences. Central and good value.

$$-$ Hostal Casa Balche
Calle 57 No 6, T981-811 0087, www.casabalche.com.
A bit more expensive than your usual hostel, but very new, comfortable, stylish and unique, and a superb location overlooking the plaza. There's just 1 private room (**$$**) and a few small clean dorms with bunks. Services include free Wi-Fi, breakfast and laundry. Attractive, hospitable and recommended.

$ Viatger Inn
Calle 51 No 28, between Calles 12 and 14, T981-811 4500, www.viatgerinn.com.
A small, crisp, clean and stylish youth hostel with mixed and single-sex dorms. Coffee and Wi-Fi included. Brand new and in great shape.

Restaurants

Campeche is known for its seafood, especially *camarones* (large shrimps), *esmedregal* (black snapper) and *pan de cazón* (baby hammerhead shark sandwiched between corn tortillas with black beans). Food stands in the market serve *tortas*, tortillas, *panuchos* and *tamales* but hygiene standards vary widely; barbecued venison is also a marketplace speciality.

$$$ Anchor's 59
Calle 59 between Calles 10 and 12.
A plush new seafood restaurant, recommended chiefly for its stock of wine. Smart, pleasant interior and a tempting menu of grilled coconut prawns, seafood tostadas, snapper, pasta and more.

$$$ Don Gustavo
Calle 59 No 4, T01800-839 0959, www.casadongustavo.com.
Don Gustavo's is the place for a romantic evening meal. They serve creatively prepared local specialities, steaks, pasta and fusion cuisine. The setting, inside the hotel, is a handsome colonial house with an elegant dining room and intimate patio seating. Attentive service.

$$$ La Pigua
Av Miguel Alemán 179A, www.lapigua.com.mx.
La Pigua is well-established, modern and clean. It has a traditional kitchen specializing in fresh fish, prawn cocktails, calamari, Campeche caviar and other seafood. Pleasant dining, open for lunch and dinner.

$$$-$$ Ambigú
Calle 59 between Calles 10 and 12.
A cool place with a friendly atmosphere and a simple but elegant interior and additional al fresco seating on the pedestrian street. They serve home-cooked regional cuisine and great cocktails made with traditional plants, fruits and nance liquor.

$$$-$$ El Bastión de Campeche
Calle 57 No 2a, www.elbastion.mx.
A good spot on the plaza, clean and pleasant. They serve Mexican, Yucatec and international cuisine, specialities include chicken stuffed with cream cheese and chaya, filet mignon and shrimp in mango sauce. Breakfast, lunch and dinner.

$$$-$$ Luz de Luna
Calle 59 No 6, between Calles 10 and 12.
A good Mexican restaurant serving national and local classics, including flavourful burritos, tacos, enchiladas and fish fillet with lemon and pepper. Friendly, attentive service and al fresco seating.

$$$-$$ Marganzo
Calle 8, www.marganzo.com.
Highly regarded by the locals, **Marganzo** is a colonial-style restaurant serving good seafood and Mexican fare, including Yucatec specialities. They regularly lay on music with a trio of musicians and regional dancing. Good evening atmosphere. Recommended.

$$-$ La Parroquia
Calle 55 No 8, part of the hotel with the same name.
This busy locals' joint – staffed by smartly attired and friendly waiters – is open 24 hrs and packed at breakfast time. They serve reliable grub, reasonable and casual, but not gourmet. Free Wi-Fi.

$ Fresh 'n Green
Calle 59 No 5.
A simple sandwich and salad bar, very casual and cheap, fast food, and popular with students.

Cafés

Chocol Ha
Calle 59 No 30.
A chilled-out little patio, great for after-dinner crêpes, frappés and hot chocolate. They have some tasty local produce on sale too, including honey and chocolate.

Festivals

Feb/Mar Good **Carnival.**
7 Aug State holiday.
Sep Feria de San Román, 2nd fortnight.
4-13 Oct Fiesta de San Francisco.

Shopping

Handicrafts
Excellent cheap Panama hats (*jipis*), finely and tightly woven so hat they retain their shape even when crushed into your luggage (within reason); cheaper at the source in Becal. Handicrafts are generally cheaper than in Mérida. There are souvenir shops along Calle 8, such as **Artesanía Típica Naval**, Calle 8 No 259, with exotic bottled fruit like *nance* and *marañón*. Many high-quality craft items are available from the **Exposición** in the Baluarte San Pedro and **Casa de Artesanías Tukulná**, Calle 10 No 333, between C59 and C31, www.tukulna.com.mx, open daily 0900-2000.

The **market**, from which most local buses depart, is beside Alameda Park at the south end of Calle 57. There are plenty of bargains here. Try the ice cream, although preferably from a shop rather than a barrow.

What to do

Tour operators
Kankabi'Ok, *Calle 59 No 3, between Calles 8 and 10, T981-811 2792, www.kankabiok. com*. Eco and adventure tours, including kayaking, camping and ruins. A tour to Edzná is around US$25 per person (2-person minimum), including transport and guide. Other popular excursions include the 'Camino Real', a half-day tour of rural villages and workshops, including a traditional meal.
Viajes Xtampak Tours, *Calle 57 No 14, T981-816 6473, www.xtampak.com*. Daily transport to ruins including Edzná, Calakmul, Uxmal and Palenque – they'll collect you from your hotel with 24 hrs' notice. There's a discount for groups and guide services at an extra cost. Recommended.

Transport

Air
The modern, efficient airport (**CPE**) on Porfirio is 10 km northeast of town. If on a budget, walk 100 m down service road (Av Aviación) to Av Nacozari, turn right (west) and wait for 'China–Campeche' bus to the Zócalo.

Aeroméxico direct daily to **Mexico City**, T981-816 3109.

Bus
Long-distance buses arrive at the **ADO** bus terminal on Av Casa de Justicia 237, 3 km from downtown; buses to the centre pass outside, US$0.70, taxis cost US$3.

Buses to **Seybaplaya** leave from the tiny Cristo Rey terminal opposite the market, 9 a day from 0615, 45 mins, US$1.50.

Long distance See above for the location of the 1st-class **ADO** terminal. The 2nd-class bus terminal is about 1 km east of the centre along Av Gobernadores, but services are steadily moving to the main terminal. To **Cancún**, 8 daily with **ADO** and **ADO GL**, 7 hrs, US$38-45. To **Chetumal**, 1400, 6 hrs, US$38. To **Ciudad del Carmen**, frequent **ADO** services, 3 hrs, US$16. To **Escárcega**, 6 daily, 2 hrs, US$11. To **Mérida**, frequent **ADO** services, 2½ hrs, US$14. To **San Cristóbal de las Casas**, **OCC** at 2145, 11 hrs, US$36. To **Veracruz**, luxury only, **ADO GL** at 2010, 11½ hrs, US$62. To **Villahermosa**, frequent **ADO** services, 6-7 hrs, US$31.

Car
Car hire **Maya Nature**, Av Ruiz Cortines 51, inside Hotel del Mar, T981-811 9191. **Hertz** and **Autorent** car rentals at airport.

Mayan sites east of Campeche

little-visited sites buried in the jungle

A number of city remains (mostly in the Chenes architectural style) are scattered throughout the rainforest and scrub to the east of Campeche; little excavation work has been done and most receive few visitors. Getting to them by the occasional bus service is possible in some cases, but return trips can be tricky. The alternatives are one of the tours run by travel agencies in Campeche (see Tour operators, above) or renting a vehicle (preferably with high clearance) in Campeche or Mérida. Whichever way you travel, you are strongly advised to carry plenty of drinking water.

Edzná

Tue-Sun 0800-1700, US$3.50; local guides available. The easiest way to reach Edzná is on a tourist minibus. They depart hourly and operators include Xtampak, Calle 57 No 14, between Calle 10 and 12, T981-812 8655, xtampac_7@ hotmail.com, US$21.50 (prices drop depending on number of passengers); and Transportadora Turística Jade, Av Díaz Ordaz No 67, T981-827 4885, Jade_tour@hotmail.com, US$14. To get there on public transport, catch a morning bus to Pich and ask to be let out at Edzná – it's a 15-min walk from the highway. Ask the driver about return schedules, as services are quite infrequent and subject to change. There's no accommodation at Edzná and hitchhiking isn't recommended.

The closest site to the state capital is Edzná ('House of Grimaces'), reached by the highway east to Cayal, then a right turn onto Highway 261, a distance of 61 km. A paved shortcut southeast through China and Poyaxum (good road) cuts off 11 km; follow Avenida Nacozari out along the railway track.

Gracefully situated in a lovely, tranquil valley with thick vegetation on either side, Edzná was a huge ceremonial centre, occupied from about 600 BC to AD 200, built in the simple Chenes style mixed with Puuc, Classic and other influences. The centrepiece is the magnificent, 30-m-tall, 60-sq-m **Temple of the Five Storeys**, a stepped pyramid with four levels of living quarters for the priests and a shrine and altar at the top; 65 steep steps lead up from the Central Plaza. Opposite is the **Paal U'na**, Temple of the Moon. Excavations are being carried out on the scores of lesser temples by Guatemalan refugees under the direction of Mexican archaeologists, but most of Edzná's original sprawl remains hidden away under thick vegetation. Imagination is still needed to picture the network of irrigation canals and holding basins built by the Maya along the valley below sea level. Some of the stelae remain in position (two large stone faces with grotesquely squinting eyes are covered by a thatched shelter); others can be seen in various Campeche museums. There is also a good example of a *sacbé* (sacred road).

Edzná is well worth a visit especially in July, when a Mayan ceremony to honour Chac is held, to encourage or to celebrate the arrival of the rains (exact date varies). There is a small *comedor* at the entrance.

Hochob
Daily 0800-1700, US$2.70.

Of the more remote and less-visited sites beyond Edzná, Hochob and Dzibilnocac are the best choices for the non-specialist. Hochob is reached by turning right at Hopelchén on Highway 261, 85 km east of Campeche. This quiet town has an impressive fortified 16th-century church but only one hotel. From here a narrow paved road leads 41 km south to the village of **Dzibalchén**.

Don Willem Chan will guide tourists to Hochob (he also rents bikes), is helpful and speaks English. Directions can be obtained from the church here (run by Americans); you need to travel 18 km southwest on a good dirt road (no public transport, hopeless quagmire in the rainy season) to the village of **Chenko**, where locals will show the way (4 km through the jungle). Bear left when the road forks; it ends at a small *palapa* and, from here, the ruins are 1 km uphill with a magnificent view over the surrounding forest.

Hochob once covered a large area but, as at Edzná, only the hilltop ceremonial centre (the usual plaza surrounded by elaborately decorated temple buildings) has been properly excavated; although many of these are mounds of rubble, the site is perfect for contemplating deserted, yet accessible Mayan ruins in solitude and silence. The one-room temple to the right (north) of the plaza is the most famous structure: deep-relief patterns of stylized snakes moulded in stucco across its façade were designed to resemble a mask of the ferocious rain god Chac. A door serves as the mouth. A fine reconstruction of the building is on display at the Museo de Antropología in Mexico City. Early morning second-class buses serve Dzibalchén, but returning to Campeche later in the day is often a matter of luck.

Dzibilnocac
Daily 0800-1700, free.

Some 20 km northeast of Dzibalchén at Iturbide, this site is one of the largest in Chenes territory. Only three temples have been excavated here (many pyramidal mounds in the forest and roadside *milpas*); the first two are in a bad state of preservation, but the third is worth the visit: a unique narrow edifice with rounded corners and remains of a stucco façade, primitive reliefs and another grim mask of Chac on the top level. Much of the stonework from the extensive site is used by local farmers for huts and fences.

Several buses daily travel to Iturbide, three hours, US$6.70, and there is no accommodation. If driving your own vehicle, well-marked 'km' signs parallel the rocky road to Iturbide (no accommodation); bear right around the tiny Zócalo and its attendant yellow church and continue (better to walk in the wet season) for 50 m, where the right branch of a fork leads to the ruins. Other sites in the region require 4WD transport and appeal mostly to archaeologists.

Becal
Becal is the centre for weaving Panama hats, here called *jipis* (pronounced 'hippies') and ubiquitous throughout the Yucatán. Many of the town's families

have workshops in cool, moist backyard underground caves, which are necessary for keeping moist and pliable the shredded leaves of the *jipijapa* palm from which the hats are made. Most vendors give the visitor a tour of their workshop, but are quite zealous in their sales pitches. Prices are better for *jipis* and other locally woven items (cigarette cases, shoes, belts, etc) in the **Centro Artesanal, Artesanías de Becaleña** ⓘ *Calle 30 No 210*, than in the shops near the plaza, where the hat is honoured by a hefty sculpture of three concrete *sombreros*! More celebrations take place on 20 May during the **Feria del Jipi**.

Gulf coast
languid ports, fishing villages, mangroves, lagoons and desolate beaches

Opening to expansive views of the ocean, Campeche's Gulf Coast sweeps south from Campeche City. The Highway 180 clings to the narrow shore, crumbling into the sea in places and usually ignored by tourists, but scenic. Running parallel, the toll road connecting Campeche City to Champotón is rapid, but bypasses Seybaplaya and Sihoplaya.

Seybaplaya and Sihoplaya
The low-key Mexican resort of **Seybaplaya**, 32 km south of Campeche City, is a dusty, mellow place where fishermen mend nets and pelicans dry their wings along the beach. On the highway there are open-air restaurants serving red snapper, but in general there's little to explore. Only the **Balneario Payucán** at the north end of the bay makes a special trip worthwhile; it is the closest decent beach to Campeche, but quite isolated. A short distance further south of Seybaplaya is the smaller resort of **Sihoplaya** (regular buses from Campeche US$1).

Champotón
Run-down but relaxed, Champotón, 66 km south of Campeche City, is a fishing and shrimping port sprawled at the mouth of the Río Champotón. In pre-Hispanic times, it was an important trade link between Guatemala and Central Mexico. Toltec and Maya mingled here, followed by the Spaniards, including ill-fated Francisco Hernández de Córdoba, fatally wounded in a skirmish with the inhabitants in 1517. The remnants of the 1719 San Antonio fort, built as a defence against the pirates, can be seen the south side of town. The **Feast of the Immaculate Conception** (8 December) is celebrated with a joyous festival lasting several days. At Champotón, Highway 261 runs 86 km due south to Escárcega, joining Highway 186, giving access to southern Campeche State and Chetumal in Quintana Roo.

Ciudad del Carmen
Perched between the Gulf of Mexico and Laguna de Términos (named during the first Spanish expedition when it thought it had reached the end of the 'island' of Yucatán), Ciudad del Carmen is the hot, bursting-at-the-seams principal oil port of the region.

The site was established in 1588 by a pirate named McGregor, as a lair from which to raid Spanish shipping; it was infamous until the pirates were wiped out in 1717 by Alfonso Felipe de Andrade, who named the town after its patroness, the Virgen del Carmen. The patroness is honoured with a cheerful fiesta each year between 15 and 30 June.

The attractive, cream-coloured **cathedral** (Parroquia de la Virgen del Carmen), begun 1856, is notable for its stained glass. **La Iglesia de Jesús** (1820) opposite Parque Juárez is surrounded by elegant older houses. Nearby is the Barrio del Guanal, the oldest residential quarter, with the church of the **Virgen de la Asunción** (1815) and houses with spacious balconies and tiles brought from Marseille. There are several good beaches with restaurants and water sports, the most scenic being **Playa Caracol** (southeast of the centre) and **Playa Norte**, which has extensive white sand and is safe for bathing. The lagoon is rich in tarpon (*sábalo*) and bonefish.

West of Ciudad del Carmen

A few kilometres west of Ciudad del Carmen, the **Zacatal** bridge crosses the lagoon to connect with the mainland; at 3.2 km it is the longest bridge in Latin America (celebrated with a light and sound show every evening). Near the exit, the lighthouse of **Xicalango** stands at the site of an important pre-Columbian trading centre. Cortés landed near here in 1519 on his way to Veracruz and was given 20 female slaves, including 'La Malinche', the indigenous princess baptized as Doña Marina who, as the Spaniards' interpreter, played an important role in the Conquest. A series of lagoons lie further west on Highway 180, good for birdwatching. Thereafter, the highway crosses the state border into Tabasco, skirting the Gulf up to the US border.

Listings Ciudad del Carmen

Where to stay

Hotel accommodation is generally poor value and can be difficult to come by Mon-Thu; book in advance and arrive early. You'll find a handful of 'economical' hotels opposite the ADO bus station.

$$$ EuroHotel
Calle 22 No 208, T938-382 3044, reganem@prodigy.net.mx.
Large and modern, 2 restaurants, pool, a/c, disco, built to accommodate the flow of Pemex traffic.

$ Lino's
Calle 31 No 132, T938-382 0788.
A/c, pool, restaurant, also has 10 RV spaces with electricity hook-ups.

Restaurants

$$ El Kiosco Calle 33 s/n
Between Calle 20 and 22, in Hotel del Parque with view of the Zócalo.
Modest prices, eggs, chicken, seafood and Mexican dishes.

$$-$ El Pavo
Tucked away down Calle 36A, in Col Guadalupe.
This superb, family-run restaurant serves excellent seafood dishes at cheap prices. Very popular with the locals.

$$-$ La Fuente
Calle 20.
24-hr snack bar with view of the Laguna.

$ La Mesita
Outdoor stand across from the old ferry landing.
Well-prepared shrimp, seafood cocktails, extremely popular all day.

Transport

Air
Carmen's airport (**CME**, 5 km east of the plaza) currently only has direct flights to **Mexico City**, from where there are connections to the rest of the country.

Bus
The **ADO** bus terminal is some distance from the centre. Take bus or *colectivo* marked 'Renovación' or 'ADO'; they leave from around the Zócalo. There are frequent **ADO** and **ATS** services to **Campeche**, 2½-3 hrs, US$16. To **Mérida**, frequent, 6 hrs, US$29. To **Villahermosa** via the coast, 3 hrs, US$14, where connections can be made to **Palenque**. Buses also travel via **Escárcega**, where you can connect to **Chetumal** and **Belize**.

Car
Car hire Budget, Calle 31 No 117, T938-382 0908. **Auto-Rentas del Carmen**, Calle 33 No 121, T938-382 2376.

Southern Campeche

a remote forested area concealing scores of unexplored Mayan ruins

This region encompasses part of the vast lowland forest that reaches into northern Guatemala's Petén, much of it inaccessible without a guide and a good machete. For vehicles, the Escárcega–Chetumal highway bisects the region and eventually connects with Chetumal in Quintana Roo. From the hamlet of Xpujil, 150 km east of Escárcega, you can access the sites of Xpujil, Becán and Chicanná, all intriguing examples of the Río Bec architectural style, which is characterized by heavy masonry towers simulating pyramids and temples, usually found rising in pairs at the ends of elongated buildings. Encompassing a densely forested wilderness, the Calakmul Biosphere Reserve is an exceptional destination, home to one of the most powerful capitals in Mayan history, a site of monumental proportions.

Francisco Escárcega

The town of Francisco Escárcega grew up on the Coatzacoalcos–Mérida railway line, which once transported the state's bounty of precious wood, rubber and gum. Today, at the junction of Highways 261 and 186, it is a major hub for travellers on their way to and from Mayan sites in southern Campeche, as well as south to Tabasco and Chiapas and north to Campeche City. The town itself is not particularly enticing, set on a busy highway with a dusty Wild West atmosphere. If stuck here overnight, there are a few hotels, a bank and several cheap restaurants (see Listings, below).

★Calakmul

Daily 0800-1700, US$3.70, cars US$4, entrance to biosphere reserve US$4. Calakmul is only accessible by car; take Route 186 until Km 95, then turn off at Conhuás, where a paved road leads to the site, 60 km.

Some 300 km southeast from Campeche town and a further 60 km off the main Escárcega–Chetumal road are the ruins of Calakmul. The site has been the subject of much attention in recent years, due to the previously concealed scale of the place. It is now believed to be one of the largest archaeological sites in Mesoamerica, and certainly the biggest of all the Mayan cities, with somewhere in the region of 10,000 buildings in total, many of them as yet unexplored. The scale of the site is vast and many buildings are still under excavation, which means that information on Calakmul's history is continually being updated. There is evidence that Calakmul was begun in 300 BC, and continually added to until AD 800.

At the centre of the site is the **Gran Plaza**, overlooked by Structure II, a massive 45-m-high pyramid built in several phases; its core dates to the middle pre-Classic era (200-400 BC) with numerous reconstructions and layers added over the centuries until the end of the Classic era (AD 900). One of the buildings grouped around the Gran Plaza is believed, due to its curious shape and location, to have been designed for astronomical observation. The **Gran Acrópolis**, the largest of all the structures, is divided into two sections: **Plaza Norte**, with the ball court, was used for ceremonies; **Plaza Sur** was used for public activities.

Chicanná
Daily 0800-1700. US$3.40.

Located 12 km from Xpujil, Chicanná was named upon its discovery in 1966 in reference to Structure II: *chi* (mouth), *can* (serpent) and *ná* (house), 'House of the Serpent's Mouth'. Due to its dimensions and location, Chicanná is considered to have been a small residential centre for the rulers of the ancient regional capital of Becán. It was occupied during the late pre-Classic period (300 BC-AD 250); the final stages of activity at the site have been dated to the post-Classic era (AD 1100). Typical of the Río Bec style are numerous representations of the Maya god Itzamná, or Earth Mother. One of the temples has a dramatic entrance in the shape of a monster's mouth, with fangs jutting out over the lintel and more fangs lining the access stairway. A taxi will take you from Xpujil bus stop to Becán and Chicanná for US$10, including waiting time.

Becán
Daily 0800-1700, US$3.70.

Seven kilometres west of Xpujil, Becán is another important site in the Río Bec style. Its most outstanding feature is a moat, now dry, which surrounds the entire city and is believed to be one of the oldest defence systems in Mesoamerica. Seven entrance gates cross the moat to the city. The large variety of buildings on the site are a strange combination of decorative towers and fake temples, as well as structures used as shrines and palaces. The twin towers, typical of the Río Bec style, feature on the main structure, set on a pyramid-shaped base supporting a cluster of buildings that seem to have been used for many different functions.

Xpujil
Tue-Sun 0800-1700, US$3.40, US$3 to use a camcorder. To get there, see Transport, below.

The name means a type of plant similar to a cattail. The main building at Xpujil features an unusual set of three towers, with rounded corners and steps that are so steep they are unscalable, suggesting they may have been purely decorative. The façade features the open jaws of an enormous reptile in profile on either side of the main entrance, possibly representing Itzamná, the Maya god of creation. Xpujil's main period of activity was AD 500-750; it began to go into decline around 1100. Major excavation on the third structure was done as recently as 1993, and there are still many unexcavated buildings dotted about the site. It can be very peaceful and quiet in the early mornings, compared with the throng of tourist activity at the more accessible sites such as Chichén Itzá and Uxmal.

Hormiguero

Daily 0800-1700, free.

Some 20 km southwest of Xpujil, Hormiguero is the site of one of the most important buildings in the Río Bec region, whose elaborate carvings on the façade show a fine example of the serpent's-mouth entrance, with huge fangs and a gigantic eye.

Río Bec

Río Bec is south off the main highway, some 10 km further along the road to Chetumal. Although the site gave its name to the architectural style seen in this area, there are better examples of the style at the ruins listed above. Río Bec is a cluster of numerous small sites, all of which are difficult to reach without a guide.

Listings Southern Campeche

Where to stay

Francisco Escárcega

$$ Escárcega
Justo Sierra 86, T982-824 0187, around the corner from the bus terminal (turn left twice).
Clean, bath, parking, hot water, good restaurant, small garden.

$$ María Isabel
Justo Sierra 127, T982-824 0045.
A/c, restaurant, comfortable, back rooms noisy from highway.

Restaurants

Francisco Escárcega

There are few places used to serving tourists, but there is a good and cheap *lonchería* opposite the bus terminal.

$$ Titanic
Corner of the main highway and the road to the train station (1st turning on the right after turning right out of the bus terminal).
For a more expensive meal with a/c.

Transport

Francisco Escárcega
Bus
Most buses from Chetumal or Campeche drop you off at the 2nd-class terminal on the main highway. To buy tickets, you have to wait until the outgoing bus has arrived; sit near the ticket office and wait for them to call out your destination, then join the scrum at the ticket office. There is an **ADO** terminal west of the 2nd-class terminal, a 20-min walk. From there, 1st-class buses go to **Palenque**, 5 daily, 3-4 hrs, US$15. To **Chetumal**, 7 daily, 4 hrs, US$18. To **Campeche**, 9 daily, 2 hrs, US$11. To **Mérida**, frequent, 4½ hrs, US$24.

From the 2nd-class terminal, there are buses to **Campeche**, 16 a day, 2½ hrs, US$8. To **Chetumal**, 7 daily, 4 hrs, US$15. To **Playas de Catazajá**, connecting with *colectivos* to **Palenque**, frequent, US$7. To **Villahermosa**, 12 a day, 4 hrs, US$16. *Colectivos* to **Palenque** leave from outside the 2nd-class terminal, US$11.

Xpujil

You are strongly advised to use your own transport when exploring southern Campeche as passing buses on Highway 186 (Escárcega–Chetumal) are infrequent (every 3-4 hrs). From Xpujil, you must hire a taxi to visit the ruins.

Bus

2nd-class buses from **Chetumal** and **Escárcega** stop on the highway in the centre of Xpujil, some 800 m east of the 2 hotels. There are 4 buses a day to **Escárcega**, between 1030 and 1500, 3 hrs, US$8. 8 buses a day to **Chetumal**, 2 hrs, US$7. Change at Escárcega for buses to **Palenque** or **Campeche**. 1st-class buses will not stop at Xpujil.

Background Yucatán Peninsula

Regional history.............123
Yucatán Peninsula
    History 128
    Culture 130
    Land and environment 131
    Wildlife....................131

Regional history

While controversy exists around the precise date humans arrived in the Americas, the current prevailing view suggests the first wave of emigrants travelled across the Bering Strait ice bridge created in the last Ice Age between Siberia and Alaska approximately 15,000 years ago. Small groups of peoples quickly moved through the region as the migratory lifestyle of the hunter-gather explored the Americas. In fertile lands the development of farming and the reduced reliance on hunting and migrating encouraged groups to settle. By 1500 BC villages were developing and growing in many parts of the Americas.

Pre-Columbian civilizations

The Aztec Empire that Spanish conqueror Hernán Cortés encountered in 1519 and subsequently destroyed was the third major power to have dominated what is now known as Mexico. Before it, the empires of Teotihuacán and Tula each unified what had essentially been an area of separate indigenous groups. All three, together with their neighbours such as the Maya (dealt with below) and their predecessors, belong to a more or less common culture called Mesoamerica. Despite the wide variety of climates and terrains that fall within Mesoamerica's boundaries, from northern Mexico to El Salvador and Honduras, the civilizations that developed were interdependent, sharing the same agriculture (based on maize, beans and squash) and many sociological features. They also shared an enormous pantheon, with the god of rain and the feathered serpent-hero predominant; the offering of blood to the gods, from oneself and from sacrificial victims usually taken in war; pyramid-building; a team game played with a rubber ball; trade in feathers, jade and other valuable objects, possibly from as far away as the Andean region of South America; hieroglyphic writing; astronomy; and an elaborate calendar.

The Mesoamerican calendar was a combination of a 260-day almanac year and the 365-day solar year. A given day in one of the years would only coincide with that in the other every 52 years, a cycle called the Calendar Round. In order to give the Calendar Round a context within a larger timescale, a starting date for both years was devised; the date chosen by the Classic Maya was equivalent to 3113 BC in Christian time. Dates measured from this point are called Long Count dates. Historians divide Mesoamerican civilizations into three periods, the pre-Classic, which lasted until about AD 300, the Classic, until AD 900, and the post-Classic, from 900 until the Spanish conquest. An alternative delineation is: Olmec, Teotihuacán and Aztec, named after the dominant civilizations within each of those periods.

Olmecs

Who precisely the Olmecs were, where they came from and why they disappeared, is a matter of debate. It is known that they flourished from about 1400-400 BC, that they lived in the Mexican Gulf coast region between Veracruz and Tabasco, and that all later civilizations have their roots ultimately in Olmec culture. They carved colossal heads, stelae (tall, flat monuments), jade figures and altars; they gave great importance to the jaguar and the serpent in their imagery; they built large ceremonial centres such as San Lorenzo and La Venta. Possibly derived from the Olmecs and gaining importance in the first millennium BC was the centre in the Valley of Oaxaca at Monte Albán. This was a major city, with certain changes of influence, right through until the end of the Classic period. Also derived from the Olmecs was the Izapa civilization, on the Pacific border of present-day Mexico and Guatemala. The progression from the Olmec to the Maya civilization seems to have taken place here with obvious connections in artistic style, calendar use, ceremonial architecture and the transformation of the Izapa long-lipped god into the Maya long-nosed god.

Teotihuacán

Almost as much mystery surrounds the origins of Teotihuacán as those of the Olmecs. Teotihuacán, 'the place where men become gods', was a great urban state, holding in its power most of the Central Highlands of Mexico. Its influence can be detected in the Maya area, Oaxaca and the civilizations on the Gulf coast that succeeded the Olmecs. The monuments in the city itself, which still stands beyond the outskirts of Mexico City, are enormous, the planning precise; it is estimated that by the seventh century AD some 125,000 people were living in its immediate vicinity. Early evidence did not suggest Teotihuacán's power was gained by force, but research indicates both human sacrifice and sacred warfare took place. For reasons unknown, Teotihuacán's influence over its neighbours ended around 600 AD. Its glory coincided with that of the Classic Maya, but the latter's decline occurred some 300 years later, at which time a major change affected all Mesoamerica.

Toltecs

The start of the post-Classic period, between the Teotihuacán and Aztec horizons, was marked by an upsurge in militarism. In the semi-deserts to the north of the settled societies of central Mexico and Veracruz lived groups of nomadic hunters. These people, who were given the general name of Chichimecs, began to invade the central region and were quick to adopt the urban characteristics of the groups they overthrew. The Toltecs of Tula were one such invading force, rapidly building up an empire stretching from the Gulf of Mexico to the Pacific in central Mexico. Infighting by factions within the Toltecs split the rulers and probably hastened the empire's demise sometime after 1150. The exiled leader Topíltzin Quetzalcóatl (Feathered Serpent) is possibly the founder of the Maya-Toltec rule in the Yucatán (the Maya spoke of a Mexican invader named Kukulcán – Feathered Serpent). He is certainly the mythical figure the Aztec ruler, Moctezuma II, took Cortés to be, returning by sea from the east.

Zapotecs and Mixtecs

Another important culture to develop in the first millennium AD was the Mixtec, in western Oaxaca. The Mixtecs infiltrated all the territory held by the Zapotecs, who had ruled Monte Albán during the Classic period and had built many other sites in the Valley of Oaxaca, including Mitla. The Mixtecs, in alliance with the Zapotecs, successfully withstood invasion by the Aztecs.

Aztecs

The process of transition from semi-nomadic hunter-gathering to city and empire-building continued with the Aztecs, who bludgeoned their way into the midst of rival city states in the vacuum left by the destruction of Tula around 1150. They rose from practically nothing to a power almost as great as Teotihuacán in about 200 years. From their base at Tenochtitlán in Lake Texcoco in the Valley of Mexico they aggressively extended their sphere of influence from the Tarascan Kingdom in the north to the Maya lands in the south. Not only did the conquered pay heavy tribute to their Aztec overlords, but they also supplied the constant flow of sacrificial victims needed to satisfy the deities, at whose head was Huitzilopochtli, the warrior god of the Sun. The speed with which the Aztecs adapted to a settled existence and fashioned a highly effective political state is remarkable. Their ability in sculpting stone, in pottery, in writing books, and in architecture (what we can gather from what the Spaniards did not destroy) was great. Surrounding all this activity was a strictly ritual existence, with ceremonies and feasts dictated by the two enmeshing calendars. It is impossible to say whether the Aztec Empire would have gone the way of its predecessors had the Spaniards not arrived to precipitate its collapse. Undoubtedly, the Europeans received much assistance from people who had been oppressed by the Aztecs and who wished to be rid of them. Within two years Cortés, with his horses, an array of military equipment and relatively few soldiers, brought to an end an extraordinary culture.

Maya

The best known of the pre-Conquest indigenous civilizations of the present Central American area was the Maya, thought to have evolved in a formative period in the Pacific highlands of Guatemala and El Salvador between 1500 BC and about 100 AD. After 200 years of growth it entered what is known today as its Classic period when the civilization flourished in Guatemala, El Salvador, Belize, Honduras and Mexico (Chiapas, Campeche and Yucatán). The Maya civilization was based on independent and antagonistic city states, including Tikal, Uaxactún, Kaminaljuyú, Iximché, Zaculeu and Quiriguá in Guatemala; Copán in Honduras; Altun Ha, Caracol, Lamanai in Belize; Tazumal and San Andrés in El Salvador; and Palenque, Bonampak (both in Chiapas), Uxmal, Mayapán, Tulum, Cobá and the Puuc hill cities of Sayil, Labná and Kabah (all on the Yucatán Peninsula) in Mexico. Recent research has revealed that these cities, far from being the peaceful ceremonial centres once imagined, were warring adversaries, striving to capture victims for sacrifice. Furthermore, much of the cultural activity, controlled by a theocratic minority of priests and nobles, involved blood-letting, by even the highest members of society. Royal blood was the most precious offering that could be made to the gods. This change in perception of the Maya was the result of the discovery of defended cities and of a greater understanding of the Maya's hieroglyphic writing. Although John Lloyd Stephens' prophecy that "a key surer than that of the Rosetta stone will be discovered" has not yet been fulfilled, the painstaking decipherment of the glyphs has uncovered many secrets of Maya society (see *Breaking the Maya Code* by Michael D Coe, Thames and Hudson).

Alongside the preoccupation with blood was an artistic tradition rich in ceremony, folklore and dance. They achieved paper codices and glyphic writing, which also appears on stone monuments and their fine ceramics; they were skilful weavers and traded over wide areas, though they did not use the wheel and had no beasts of burden. The cities were all meticulously dated. Maya art is a mathematical art: each column, figure, face, animal, frieze, stairway and temple expresses a date or a time relationship. When, for example, an ornament on the ramp of the Hieroglyphic Stairway at Copán was repeated some 15 times, it was to express that number of elapsed 'leap' years. The 75 steps stand for the number of elapsed intercalary days. The Maya calendar was a nearer approximation to sidereal time than either the Julian or the Gregorian calendars of Europe; it was only .000069 of a day out of true in a year. They used the zero centuries in advance of the Old World, plotted the movements of the sun, moon, Venus and other planets, and conceived a cycle of more than 1800 million days.

Their tools and weapons were flint and hard stone, obsidian and fire-hardened wood, and yet with these they hewed out and transported great monoliths over miles of difficult country, and carved them over with intricate glyphs and figures that would be difficult enough with modern chisels. Also with those tools they grew lavish crops. To support urban populations now believed to number tens of thousands, and a population density of 150 per sq km (compared with less than one per sq km today), an agricultural system was developed of raised fields, fertilized by fish and vegetable matter from surrounding canals. The height of the Classic period lasted until AD 900-1000, after which the Maya concentrated into Yucatán after a successful invasion of their other lands by non-Maya people (this is only one theory; another is that they were forced to flee due to drought and a peasant rebellion). They then came under the influence of the Toltecs who invaded Yucatán (Chichén Itzá is seen as an example of a Maya city that displays many Toltec features). From then on their culture declined. The Toltecs gradually spread their empire as far as the southern borders of Guatemala. They in turn were conquered by the Aztecs, who did not penetrate Central America.

Conquest and colonial rule

The remarkable conquest of Mexico began when 34-year-old Hernán Cortés disembarked near the present port of Veracruz with about 500 men, some horses and cannon, on 21 April 1519. They marched into the interior, arrived at the Aztec capital of Tenochtitlán in November and were admitted into the city as guests of the reigning monarch, Moctezuma. There they remained until June of the next year, when Pedro de Alvarado, in the absence of Cortés, murdered hundreds of natives to quell his own fear of a rising. At this treacherous act they did in fact rise, and it was only by luck that the Spanish troops, with heavy losses, were able to fight their way out of the city on the Noche Triste (the Night of Sorrows) of 30 June. The following year Cortés came back with reinforcements and besieged the city. It fell on 30 August 1521, and was utterly razed. Cortés then turned to the conquest of the rest of the country. One of the main factors in his success was his alliance with the Tlaxcalans, old rivals of the Aztecs. The fight was ruthless, the Aztecs were soon overcome and 300 years of Spanish rule followed.

Under Pedro de Alvarado the *encomienda* system was introduced whereby the Maya were forced to work land that was previously theirs and pay tribute to the colonialists in the form of crops. In return they received Christian instruction. They were treated like slaves and gradually died in their thousands from Western diseases.

Settlement and economy

The groups of Spanish settlers were few and widely scattered, a fundamental point in explaining the political fragmentation of Central America today. Panama was ruled from Bogotá, but the rest of Central America was subordinate to the Viceroyalty at Mexico City, with Antigua, Guatemala, as an Audiencia for the area until 1773, and thereafter Guatemala City. The small number of Spaniards intermarried freely with the locals, accounting for the predominance of mestizos in present-day Central America.

In the early years of colonial rule, Spanish grandees stepped into the shoes of dead Aztec lords and inherited their great estates, soon to be integrated into the *hacienda* system with its absolute title to the land and almost feudal way of life. Within the first 50 years, all the *indígenas* in the populous southern valleys of the plateau had been Christianized and harnessed for the economy. By the end of the 16th century, the Spaniards had founded most of the towns that are still important, tapped great wealth in mining, stock raising and sugar-growing, and firmly imposed their way of life and beliefs. Government was by a Spanish-born upper class, based on the subordination of the *indígena* and mestizo populations and there was a strict dependence on Spain for all things. As with the rest of Hispanic America, Spain excluded from government both Spaniards born in Mexico and the small body of educated *mestizos*, a policy which eventually led to rebellion.

Independence and nationhood

In Mexico, the standard of revolt was raised in 1810 by the curate of Dolores, Miguel Hidalgo. The *Grito de Dolores* (*Mueran los gachupines* – Perish the Spaniards), collected 80,000 armed supporters, and had it not been for Hidalgo's loss of nerve and failure to engage the Spaniards, the capital might have been captured in the first month. For the next decade, fighting across the region ensued, creating bitter differences. It was the revolution of 1820 in Spain itself that finally precipitated independence. On 24 February 1821, a loyalist general turned rebel, Agustín de Iturbide, proclaimed an independent Mexico with his Plan de Iguala and later assumed the title of Emperor Agustín I.

Yucatán Peninsula

History

The nation of Mexico was formally created on 4 October 1824, with General Guadalupe Victoria as president. Conservatives stood for a highly centralized government; Liberals favoured federated sovereign states. The tussle of interests resulted in endemic civil war. In 1836, Texas, whose cotton-growers and cattle-ranchers had been infuriated by the abolition of slavery in 1829, rebelled against the dictator, Santa Ana, and declared its Independence. It was annexed by the United States in 1845. War broke out and US troops occupied Mexico City in 1847. Next year, under the terms of the treaty of Guadalupe Hidalgo, the US acquired half Mexico's territory: all the land from Texas to California and from the Río Grande to Oregon.

Benito Juárez

A period of liberal reform dominated by independent Mexico's great hero, the Zapoteco, Benito Juárez, began in 1857. The church, in alliance with the conservatives, hotly contested his programme and the constant civil strife wrecked the economy. Juárez was forced to suspend payment on the national debt, causing the French to invade and occupy Mexico City in 1863. They imposed the Archduke Maximilian of Austria as Mexican Emperor, but under US pressure, withdrew their troops in 1867. Maximilian was captured by the Juaristas at Querétaro, tried, and shot on 19 June. Juárez resumed control of the country and died in July 1872.

General Porfirio Díaz

Sebastián Lerdo de Tejada, the distinguished scholar who followed Juárez, was soon tricked out of office by General Porfirio Díaz, who ruled Mexico from 1876 to 1910. Díaz's paternal, though often ruthless, central authority introduced a period of 35 years of peace. A superficial prosperity followed, but the main mass of peasants had never been so wretched. It was this open contradiction between dazzling prosperity and hideous distress that led to the start of civil war (known as the Mexican Revolution) in November 1910, and to Porfirio Díaz's self-exile in Paris.

The Mexican Revolution

A new leader, Francisco Madero, championed a programme of political and social reform, which included the restoration of stolen lands. Madero was initially supported by revolutionary leaders such as Emiliano Zapata in Morelos, Pascual Orozco in Chihuahua and Pancho Villa, also in the north. During his presidency (1911-1913), Madero neither satisfied his revolutionary supporters, nor pacified his reactionary enemies. After a coup in February 1913, led by General Victoriano Huerta, Madero was brutally murdered, but the great cry, 'Tierra y Libertad' (Land and Freedom) was not to be quieted until the election of Alvaro Obregón to the Presidency in 1920. Before then, Mexico was in a state of civil war, leading first to the exile of Huerta in 1914, then the dominance of Venustiano Carranza's revolutionary faction over that of Zapata (assassinated in 1919) and Villa.

The PRI

In 1946, the official ruling party assumed the name Partido Revolucionario Institucional (PRI), and held a virtual monopoly over all political activity. In the late 1980s, disaffected PRI members and others formed the breakaway Partido de la Revolución Democrática (PRD), which rapidly gained support. On New Year's Day of the election year, 1994, at the moment when the North American Free Trade Agreement (NAFTA) came into force, a guerrilla group, The Ejército Zapatista de Liberación Nacional (EZLN) briefly took control of several towns in Chiapas. Despite ongoing unrest, PRI candidate Ernesto Zedillo Ponce de León, a US-trained economist and former education minister, won a comfortable majority in the August elections.

Ernesto Zedillo

On 20 December, just after his inauguration, Zedillo devalued the peso, claiming that political unrest was causing capital outflows. On 22 December a precipitate decision to allow the peso to float against the dollar caused an immediate crisis of confidence and investors in Mexico lost billions of dollars as the peso's value plummeted. Mexicans were hard hit by the recession and the ruling position of the PRI was damaged. In Chiapas, Zedillo suspended the controversial PRI governor, but the tension between the EZLN and the army continued as a 72-hour campaign to apprehend the EZLN leader, Subcomandante Marcos, failed. Talks recommenced in April, with the EZLN calling a ceasefire but the first peace accord was not signed until February 1996. Mid-term congressional elections held in July 1997 showed the PRI's grip on power was beginning to fade. They suffered a huge blow at the polls, and for the first time ever it lost control of Congress, winning only 239 seats. The PRD surged to become the second largest party in the lower house, with 125 deputies, while the right-wing PAN won 122.

Vicente Fox

During the 1999 presidential elections, Zedillo relinquished his traditional role in nominating his successor and the PRI had a US-style primary election to select a candidate. The PAN, meanwhile, chose former Coca-Cola executive Vicente Fox to lead their campaign. On 2 July 1999, Mexicans gave power to Fox, former governor of Guanajuato, and the PAN, prising it from the PRI for the first time in 71 years. An admirer of 'third way' politics and of ex-US President Bill Clinton and UK Prime Minister Tony Blair, Fox took office on 1 December 2000 announcing czar-led initiatives that would tackle government corruption, drug-trafficking, crime and poverty, and the economic conditions that drive migration to the US. He proved to be a personable, if ineffectual president. One critic dismissively said Fox was "90% image and 10% ideas".

Felipe Calderón

Elections in July 2006 saw a new president leading Mexico. A close and ill-fought electoral result gave Felipe Calderón, the candidate of the ruling conservative National Action Party (PAN) a narrow win over Andrés Manuel López Obrador of the centre-left Party of the Democratic Revolution (PRD), pushing Roberto Madrazo of the Institutional Revolutionary Party (PRI) into third place. Calderón came to power looking to reduce poverty, violence, tax evasion, corruption and his own salary by 10%. Public infrastructure projects on roads, airports, bridges and dams would also intend to stem outward migration of Mexico's workforce. Ultimately, however, Calderón's term was dominated by his extremely bloody war on drugs, which began on 11 December 2006 with the dispatch of 6500 troops to Michoacán, and rapidly escalated to the involve 45,000 soldiers nationwide, along with state and federal police. Despite the military-led crack-downs against the cartels and high-profile arrests of corrupt political stooges, Calderón's war failed to stem the flow of cocaine over the US border – or the flow of weapons from the opposite direction. The official death toll at the close of Calderón's administration in 2012 was 60,000, but some estimates put the figure twice as high, excluding the 27,000 who have gone missing.

Return of the PRI

Amid civic protests and accusations of electoral fraud, Enrique Peña Nieto, a telegenic PRI candidate and former governor of Mexico state, was elected to office with 38% of the vote. Many feared a return to the old-school corruption and repression that so characterized former PRI administrations, despite Peña Nieto's smooth reassurances that his party, unlike the ineffectual PAN, knows how to govern. To date, his most significant act has been the liberalization of Mexico's energy sector, which is likely to culminate in the privatization of the national oil company, Pemex. Meanwhile, the war on drugs has continued to claim lives. In September 2014, 43 male students from the Teachers' College of Ayotzinapa, Guerrero, who had been commandeering buses to attend a march, were arrested by local police at the behest of the mayor and his wife, handed over to a local drug cartel and, according to subsequent confessions, driven to a remote garbage dump, summarily executed and incinerated. Illustrating the on-going collusion between political and criminal groups in Mexico, the incident has sparked fury and nationwide protests.

Culture

About 9% of the Mexican population are considered white, about 30% *indígena* (indigenous); with about 60% *mestizos*, a mixture in varying proportions of Spanish and *indígena*. Mexico also has infusions of Europeans, Arabs and Chinese. There is a national cultural prejudice in favour of the indigenous rather than the Spanish element, though this does not prevent indígena from being looked down on by the more Hispanic elements. There is hardly a single statue of Cortés in the whole of Mexico, although he does figure, pejoratively, in the frescoes of Diego

Rivera and his contemporaries. On the other hand the two last Aztec emperors, Moctezuma and Cuauhtémoc, are national heroes.

Indigenous peoples

The Maya are not a homogenous group, but a complex family comprised by numerous distinct ethnicities, each with their own language. The Yucatec Maya, occupying the Yucatán Peninsula, number some 2.45 million (with 892,723 Yucatec speakers) and are Mexico's biggest indigenous group after the Nahuas. They speak a single language with many distinct (but mutually intelligible) regional dialects, and lead lives with differing degrees of modernity.

Land & environment

The Yucatán is a limestone platform, a feature that rings the Gulf of Mexico all the way to Florida and is recognized as a separate chunk of the North American plate. It is comparatively flat and characterised by natural caverns, wells, sinkholes (cenotes) and white, sandy beaches. The northeast corner of Yucatán is the point nearest to Cuba and where the Caribbean Sea meets the Gulf of Mexico. It is the water passing through this passage that initiates the current known as the Gulf Stream, with its dramatic effect on the climates of Europe, thousands of miles away. It is calculated that at times, driven by strong trade winds, the surface water here is moving at as much as 6 km per hour.

Perhaps the world's most dramatic geological happening ever recorded took place in Yucatán. It is now generally agreed that the cataclysm that almost ended life on the planet 65 million years ago was a small asteroid, weighing perhaps one billion tonnes, colliding with the earth at 160,000 kph. This left a hole many kilometres deep and over 150 km wide in the Yucatán, now known as the Chicxulub Crater. This event destroyed almost everything on earth from the dinosaurs to ammonites, leaving only the most primitive organisms. Fortunately for us, life was able to re-establish itself.

Wildlife

Around three million years ago, the merging of North and South America into a single landmass sparked a mass migration of animals between both continents. Known as the Great American Faunal Interchange, it was a significant moment in the earth's natural history, heralding bold new patterns of species settlement, adaptation, predation and, in some cases, extinction. The event was accompanied by the Great American Schism, which separated the Pacific and Atlantic oceans and set marine species on their own unique evolutionary paths.

Today, southern Mexico represents the range limit for numerous North and South American animal species, as well as a land bridge for dozens of types of migratory birds. The majority of tour operators listed in this guide will offer nature-oriented tours and there are several national parks, *biotopes* or protected areas throughout the region, each with its own highlights.

Mammals

Primates are among the most easily sighted mammals in the region. Howler monkeys are noticeable for the huge row they make, especially around dawn or dusk. The spider monkey is more agile and slender and uses its prehensile tail to swing around the canopy. The smaller, white-throated capuchins are also commonly seen, moving around in noisy groups. The most frequently spotted carnivore is the white-nosed coati, a member of the racoon family, with a long snout and ringed tail. Members of the cat family are rarely seen; those in the area include the bobcat, jaguar, puma, ocelot and margay. The largest land mammal in the region is Baird's tapir, weighing up to 300 kg, but it is a forest species and very secretive. More likely to be seen are peccaries, medium-sized pig-like animals that are active both day and night. The white-tailed deer can often be spotted at dawn or dusk in drier, woodland patches. The smaller red brocket is a rainforest deer and more elusive. Rodent species you might see include the forest-dwelling agouti, which looks rather like a long-legged guinea pig. Considerably larger is the nocturnal paca, another forest species. Many species of bat are found throughout the region.

Birds

Toucans and the smaller toucanets are widespread throughout the tropical areas of the region and easy to spot. Other popular sightings include the hummingbird, frequently drawn to sugar-feeders, and the scarlet macaw. The resplendent quetzal is brilliant emerald green, with males having a bright scarlet breast and belly and long green tail streamers. The harpy eagle is extremely rare with sightings a possibility in rainforest region of southern Mexico. Other rare birds include the threatened horned guam, found only in high cloud forests. Along the coasts are masses of different seabirds, including pelicans, boobies and the magnificent frigate bird. In the coastal wetlands of the Yucután pink flamingos can be spotted.

Reptiles and amphibians

Mexico has more reptiles than any other country in the world. Snakes are rarely sighted, but if you are lucky you could see a boa constrictor curled up digesting its latest meal. In contrast, lizards are everywhere, from small geckos walking up walls in your hotel room to the large iguanas sunbathing in the tree tops. The American crocodile and spectacled caiman are both found throughout the area, with the latter being seen quite frequently. Morlet's crocodile is found only in Mexico, Belize and Guatemala. You'll certainly hear frogs and toads, even if you do not see them. However, the brightly coloured poison-dart frogs and some of the tree frogs are well worth searching out. Look for them in damp places, under logs and moist leaf litter, in rock crevices and by ponds and streams; many will be more active at night. Turtles have been nesting in the region for thousands of years; females will typically swim ashore at night, dig a nest, lay their eggs and depart. The temperature of the nest will determine the future sex of the hatchling: above 29°C female, below 29°C male. The eggs will hatch simultaneously and the young turtles will inundate the sea in an evolutionary mechanism believed to give them the best chances of survival.

Insects and spiders
There are uncounted different species of insect in the area. Probably most desirable to see are the butterflies, though some of the beetles, such as the jewel scarabs, are also pretty spectacular. If you are fascinated by spiders, look out for tarantulas, there are many different species.

Marine wildlife
The whale shark makes a seasonal migration through the coastal waters of Belize and Honduras between March and May. Less natural shark encounters can be had off Isla Mujeres, on the Yucatán, where hand-feeding brings in sting rays and nurse sharks for close but safe encounters. Marine mammals that can be sighted include whales, dolphins and manatees.

Practicalities
Cancún & Yucatán Peninsula

Getting there 135
Getting around 137
Essentials A-Z 141
Index.........................150
Credits......................152

Getting there

Air

Fares from Europe and North America peak during the northern hemisphere holiday season: 7 December to 15 January and July to mid-September. If you intend travelling during those times, book as far ahead as possible and check with an agency to find the best deal. As a rough guide a three-month London–Mexico City return in August is around US$1200. In November the same flight falls to US$1000. Travellers from Australia and New Zealand are getting an increasingly better deal compared with recent years, with special offers occasionally down to AUS$1900 flying direct to Mexico City. The more regular price is close to AUS$3200.

Fares fall into three groups, and are all on scheduled services: **Excursion** (return) fares: these have restricted validity either seven to 90 days, or seven to 180 days, depending on the airline. They are fixed-date tickets where the dates of travel cannot be changed after issue without incurring a penalty. **Yearly fares**: these may be bought on a one-way or return basis, and usually the returns can be issued with the return date left open. You must, however, fix the route. **Student** (or Under-26) fares: one way and returns available, or 'open jaws' for people intending to travel a linear route and return from a different point from that which they entered.

Airport information There are several international airports in Mexico, the two busiest are **Mexico City** and **Cancún**. If you are likely to be returning home at a busy time (eg between Christmas and New Year, or August) a booking is advisable on open-return tickets. When arriving in Mexico by air, make sure you fill in the immigration document before joining the queue to have your passport checked. Immigration formalities at Cancún international are normally very efficient. For more information see Cancún transport, page 31.

Departure tax Currently US$65 on international flights (dollars not always accepted so bring 900 pesos, cash only); always check when purchasing if departure tax is included in ticket price as it often is.

From Europe **To Mexico City**: there are several airlines that have regular direct flights. From Amsterdam with **KLM**; from Frankfurt with **Lufthansa**, **Air Berlin** and **AeroMéxico**; from London and Manchester with **British Airways** and **AeroMéxico**; from Barcelona with **Iberia**; from Madrid with **Iberia** and **AeroMéxico**; from Paris with **Air France** and **AeroMéxico**. Most connecting flights in Europe are through Madrid or Gatwick. Fares vary from airline to airline and according to time of year. Check with an agency for the best deal for when you wish to travel. **To Cancún**: from Amsterdam with **Martinair**; Dusseldorf with **Air Berlin**; Frankfurt with **Air Berlin** and Munich with **Air Berlin**; Madrid with **AeroMéxico Avianca**; and Paris with **Air France** and **American Airlines**; from London and Manchester with **British Airways**, **Virgin Atlantic**, **Thomson Flights** and **Fly Thomas Cook**.

From USA **To Mexico City**: several airlines fly this route, including **American Airlines, AeroMéxico, Delta** and **United**. Flights are available from most major cities, with the cheapest generally going through Miami, Dallas, Houston, Fort Lauderdale and sometimes Los Angeles. **To Cancún**: Flights leave from many cities across the USA. **Spirit Air** and **Jet Blue** are two no frills options.

From Canada **To Mexico City**: the options are less varied, but there are direct flights from Montreal and Toronto, as well as regular flights from other main cities. From Toronto with **United** and **Air Canada**; and from Vancouver with **Japan Airlines**. Keep an eye out for special offers, which can be extremely good value (often at very short notice).

From Australia and New Zealand From Sydney with **United** and from Auckland with **Air New Zealand**, all flying through Los Angeles.

From Latin America and the Caribbean Flights from Latin America have increased in recent years. Central America is covered by the **TACA** network, connecting the capitals of each country to Mexico City and some of the smaller regional cities. In South America, connections are to capitals and major cities. If planning a trip to Cuba there are flights from Cancún, Mérida and Mexico City with **Cubana**.

Road

From USA There are many border crossings with the US; the main ones are Tijuana, Mexicali, Nogales, Ciudad Juárez, Piedras Negras, Nuevo Laredo and Matamoros.

From Guatemala The main border town is Tapachula, with a crossing over the Talismán Bridge or at Ciudad Hidalgo. A more interesting route is via Ciudad Cuauhtémoc or heading northwest from Santa Elena/Flores towards Tenosique. There are also options for road and river travel.

From Belize The border crossing at Santa Elena is near Chetumal, where public transport can be arranged. A very quiet – and more challenging – crossing is at Blue Creek. Daily boats now connect San Pedro and Caye Caulker with Chetumal, a comparatively stress-free crossing into Mexico.

Getting around

Air

Most medium-sized towns in Mexico have an airport. If you're looking to cover a great distance in a short time, several airlines fly internal routes (a few with international flights as well) including **Aeromar** and **Aeroméxico Connect**. Low-cost airlines include: **Interjet** ⓘ *www.interjet.com.mx*, **Volaris** ⓘ *www.volaris.com.mx*, and **VivaAerobus** ⓘ *www.vivaaerobus.com*. General costs are comparable with the older airlines – you get the bargain if you can book ahead, travel at inconvenient times or if there is a special offer. **MAYAir** ⓘ www.mayair.com.mx, is a regional airline based at the new FBO terminal of Cancún International Airport; it serves Cozumel, Mérida, Veracruz and Villahermosa.

Bus *Buses are often called camiones, hence 'Central Camionero' for bus station.*

The Mexican bus system is very extensive and efficient. In some cities there is a central bus terminal (in Mexico City there are four – one at each point of the compass), in others there are a couple – one for first-class services, one for second. A third variation is division by companies. The entire network is privatized and highly competitive, although in the Yucatán, ADO and its plethora of subsidies have a virtual monopoly. Most inter-city routes are served by comfortable and very adequate first-class buses with reclining seats, air conditioning, Spanish-language movies and on-board toilet. For those seeking extra luxury, several companies offer superior class services, so-called ADO GL or Ejecutiva, which include a soft-drink, snack and almost horizontally aligned seats. It is highly advisable to book your tickets several days in advance when travelling at Christmas, Semana Santa or other national holidays. If your journey is longer than six hours, it is sensible to book 24 hours ahead. If travelling overnight, pack a sweater or blanket in your hand-luggage – the air-conditioning gets icy. Also avoid sitting near the toilet (it invariably smells).

Fares Bus travel can use up a lot of your budget. As a very rough calculation, bus travel works out at around US$5 per hour spent travelling. First-class fares are usually 10-20% dearer than second-class, the superior classes 30-40% more than first-class. Some bus tickets can be purchased at www.ticketbus.com.mx, information on T01-800-702-8000, or directly from **ADO** ⓘ *T01-800 009 9090, www.ado.com.mx*, also with timetables.

Bicycle

The Yucatán Peninsula offers plenty of enjoyable places for cycling. The main problems facing cyclists are heavy traffic, poor road conditions and a lack of specialized spare parts, particularly for mountain bikes, which can only be found in big cities. The easiest region for cycling is the Gulf of Mexico coast, but many

> **TRAVEL TIP**
>
> ### Border cooperation
>
> In June 2006, Guatemala, El Salvador, Honduras, and Nicaragua entered into a 'Central America-4 (CA-4) Border Control Agreement'. Under the terms of the agreement, citizens of the four countries may travel freely across land borders from one of the countries to any of the others without completing entry and exit formalities at immigration checkpoints. US citizens and other eligible foreign nationals, who legally enter any of the four countries, may similarly travel among the four without obtaining additional visas or tourist entry permits for the other three countries. Immigration officials at the first port of entry determine the length of stay, up to a maximum period of 90 days.

of the roads are flat and boring. The toll roads are generally preferable to the ordinary highways for cyclists; there is less traffic, more lanes and a wide paved shoulder, but take lots of water as there are few facilities. **Tip**: if you walk your bicycle on the pavement through the toll station you don't have to pay. Cycling on some main roads can be very dangerous; fit a rear-view mirror.

Car hire

Car rental is very expensive in Mexico, from US$35-45 a day for a basic model (plus 15% sales tax). The age limit is normally at least 25 and you'll need to place a deposit, normally against a credit card, for damage. It can be cheaper to arrange hire in the US or Europe. Renting a vehicle is nearly impossible without a credit card. It is twice as expensive to leave a car at a different point from the starting point than it is to make a round trip. Rates will vary from city to city. Make sure you have unlimited mileage.

Car hire insurance Check exactly what the hirer's insurance policy covers. In many cases it will only protect you against minor bumps and scrapes, not major accidents, or 'natural' damage (for example flooding). Ask if extra cover is available. Also find out, if using a credit card, whether the card automatically includes insurance. Beware of being billed for scratches that were on the vehicle before you hired it. When you return the vehicle make sure you check it with someone at the office and get signed evidence that it is returned in good condition and that you will not be charged.

In case of accident Do not abandon your vehicle. Call your insurance company immediately to inform it. Do not leave Mexico without first filing a claim. Do not sign any contract or agreement without a representative of the insurance company being present. Always carry with you, in the insured vehicle, your policy identification card and the names of the company's adjusters. A helpline for road accidents is available by phoning T02 and asking the operator to connect you to T55-5684 9715 or T55-5684 9761.

BORDER CROSSING
Mexico–Belize

Chetumal–Corozal
The main border crossing is Santa Elena for Chetumal/Corozal. Santa Elena is 12 km north of Corozal, from where there are onward connections to Belize City (three to four hours). Chetumal is 11 km north of Santa Elena and has connections to the Yucatán Peninsula and Quintana Roo beaches; see also page 72. There's a modern 24-hour immigration terminal here and formalities are usually swift. If entering Belize, it's not strictly necessary to change dollars as they are accepted everywhere at a fixed rate of 1:2. It is easier to change Mexican pesos at the border than inside Belize.

La Unión–Blue Creek
A less widely used crossing is at La Unión/Blue Creek (not recommended unless you like a challenge). There are immigration facilities here but officials are only used to dealing with Mexicans and Belizeans, so delays are likely.

Assistance Angeles Verdes (Green Angels) patrol many of Mexico's main roads. Call them toll-free on T078; every state also has an Angeles Verdes hotline. The drivers speak English, are trained to give first aid, make minor auto repairs and deal with flat tyres. Assistance is provided free of charge, you pay for the gas.

Petrol/diesel All *gasolina* is now unleaded and all petrol stations are franchised by Petróleos Mexicanos (PEMEX). Fuel costs are likely to be in flux with the floating of Pemex in 2015, approximately: regular, US$1/l; premium, US$1.07/l; diesel US$1.07. Petrol stations are not self-service; it is normal to give the attendant a small tip.

Road tolls A toll is called a *cuota*, as opposed to a non-toll road, which is a *vía libre*. There are many toll charges and the cost works out at around one peso per kilometre. Check out your route and toll prices, on the **Traza Tu Ruta** section of www.sct.gob.mx.

Warnings On all roads, if the driver flashes his lights he is claiming right of way and the oncoming traffic must give way. At *Alto* (Halt) signs, all traffic must come to a complete stop. Always avoid driving at night – night-time robberies are on the increase. 'Sleeping policemen' or road bumps can be hazardous as there are often no warning signs; they are sometimes marked *zona de topes*, or incorrectly marked as *vibradores*.

Hitchhiking
Hitchhiking in Mexico is not recommended as it is not universally safe (seek local advice). It is very easy to hitch short distances, such as the last few kilometres to an archaeological site off the main road; offer to pay something, like US$1.

Motorcycle

Motorcycling is good in southern Mexico as most main roads are in fairly good condition and hotels are usually willing to allow the bike to be parked in a courtyard or patio. In the major tourist centres, such as Playa del Carmen or Cancún, motorbike parts can be found as there are Honda dealers for bike and jet-ski rentals.

Taxi

To avoid overcharging, the government has taken control of taxi services from airports to cities. Only those with government licences are allowed to carry passengers from the airport and you can usually buy a ticket with a set price to your destination from a booth at the terminal. Tipping is not required unless the driver helps with heavy luggage or provides some extra service. Beware drivers seeking kickbacks from hotels, or you'll be charged the rack rate on check-in.

Maps

Guía Roji publish a wide range of regional maps, city plans and gazettes, available at most bookshops and news-stands. Guia Roji is online at http://guiaroji.com.mx with full street, town, city and state search facilities for the country.

Maps of the region are also published by **International Travel Maps (ITM)** ⓘ *T604-273-1400, www.itmb.com*, most with historical notes by the late Kevin Healey. An excellent source of maps in the UK is **Stanfords** ⓘ *12-14 Long Acre, Covent Garden, London, WC2E 9LP, T+44-020-7836-1321, www.stanfords.co.uk, also in Bristol.*

Essentials A-Z

Children

Travel with children can bring you into closer contact with Mexican families and generally presents no special problems; in fact, the path is often smoother for family groups. Officials tend to be more amenable where children are concerned. Always carry a copy of your child's birth certificate and passport photos. For an overview of travelling with children, visit **www.babygoes2.com**.

Transport All airlines charge a reduced price for children under 12 and less for children under 2. Double check the child's baggage allowance though; some are as low as 7 kg. On long-distance buses children generally pay half or reduced fares. For shorter trips it is cheaper, if less comfortable, to seat small children on your knee. In city and local buses, small children do not generally pay a fare, but are not entitled to a seat when paying customers are standing. On sightseeing tours you should always bargain for a family rate; often children can go free. Note that a child travelling free on a long excursion is not always covered by the operator's travel insurance.

Hotels Try to negotiate family rates. It is quite common for children under 12 to be allowed to stay for no extra charge as long as they are sharing your room.

Customs and duty free

Adults entering Mexico are allowed to bring in up to 6 litres of wine and 3 litres of spirits; 20 packs of cigarettes, or 25 cigars, or 200 g of tobacco and medicines for personal use. Goods imported into Mexico with a value of more than US$500 (with the exception of computer equipment, where the limit is US$4000) have to be handled by an officially appointed agent. If you are carrying more than US$10,000 in cash you should declare it. You may not take archaeological artefacts out of the country. Full details and latest updates are available at www.aduanas.sat.gob.mx.

Disabled travellers

Facilities for disabled travellers are severely lacking in Mexico. Most airports and hotels and restaurants in major resorts have wheelchair ramps and adapted toilets. Pavements are often in such a poor state of repair that walking is precarious.

Some travel companies specialize in exciting holidays, tailor-made for individuals depending on their level of disability. **Disabled Travelers**, www.disabledtravelers.com, provides travel information for disabled adventurers and includes a number of links, reviews and tips. You might also want to read *Nothing Ventured*, edited by Alison Walsh (Harper Collins), which gives personal accounts of worldwide journeys by disabled travellers, plus advice and listings.

Dress

Casual clothing is adequate for most occasions although men should wear trousers (not shorts) in smart restaurants (and they may need a jacket and tie for some). Dress conservatively in indigenous communities and small churches (cover your shoulders and remove your cap). Topless bathing is generally unacceptable.

Drugs

Users of drugs without medical prescription should be particularly careful, as penalties can by heavy for even the simple possession of such substances. The planting of drugs on travellers, by traffickers or the police, is not unknown. If offered drugs on the street, make no response at all and keep walking. Note that people who roll their own cigarettes are often suspected of carrying drugs and are subjected to close searches.

If you are taking illegal drugs – even ones that are widely and publically used – be aware that authorities do set traps from time to time. Should you get into trouble, your embassy is unlikely to be very sympathetic. See also Safety, page 146.

Electricity

127 volts/60 Hz, US-style 2-pin plug.

Embassies and consulates

For details of embassies in Mexico and Mexican embassies in the rest of the world, go to www.embassy.goabroad.com.

Gay and lesbian travellers

Most of Mexico and Central America is not particularly liberal in its attitudes to gays and lesbians. Having said that, times are changing and you'll find there is a gay scene with bars and clubs at least in most of the bigger cities and resorts. Helpful websites include www.gayscape.com, www.gaypedia.com and www.iglta.org (International Gay and Lesbian Travel Association).

Health

Before you go/vaccinations

See your GP or travel clinic at 4-6 weeks before departure for general advice on travel risks and vaccinations. Make sure you have sufficient medical insurance, get a dental check and know your blood group. Vaccinations are not essential to enter Mexico, but many health professionals recommend hepatitis A and typhoid for most travellers. Malaria prophylaxis is often recommended, but only really necessary if travelling in remote forested areas.

Health risks

The most common ailment for travellers to Mexico is severe **diarrhoea** known as 'Montezuma's Revenge'. If you are unfortunate enough to contract it, drink plenty of fluids and rest; consult a doctor if it persists for more than 24 hrs. Take care with drinking water, milk, uncooked vegetables and peeled fruits. Diarrhoea accompanied by vomiting is sometimes a sign of parasitic infection, usually amoebas, and you should seek immediate medical advice.

There are many insect-borne diseases in Mexico, including **dengue fever**, a not uncommon problem in poor urban areas. Mosquitoes can bite at any time of the day, but feast at dawn and dusk. Use a light repellent (jungle strength is overkill). The sun poses a significant health risk: use sun block, wear a hat and don't be deceived by an overcast sky, it won't protect you.

If you get sick
Make sure you have adequate insurance (see below). Contact your embassy or consulate for a list of doctors and dentists who speak your language, or at least some English. Good-quality healthcare is available in the larger centres but it can be expensive, especially hospitalization.

Social security hospitals are restricted to members, but will take visitors in emergencies; they are more up to date than the *Centros de Salud* and *Hospitales Civiles* found in most town centres, which are very cheap and open to everyone. A consultation in a private doctor's surgery may cost US$20-40.

Useful websites
www.btha.org   British Travel Health Association.
www.cdc.gov   US government site that gives excellent advice on travel health and details of disease outbreaks.
www.fco.gov.uk   British Foreign and Commonwealth Office travel site has useful information on each country, people, climate and a list of UK embassies/consulates.
www.fitfortravel.scot.nhs.uk   A-Z of vaccine/health advice for each country.
www.numberonehealth.co.uk   Travel screening services, vaccine and travel health advice, email/SMS text vaccine reminders and screens returned travellers for tropical diseases.

Identification

ID is increasingly required when visiting offices or tourist sites within government buildings. It's handy to have some form of identification (*identificación* or *credencial*), a photocopied passport will usually do.

Insurance

Insurance is strongly recommended and policies are very reasonable. If you have financial restraints, the most important aspect of any insurance policy is medical care and repatriation. Ideally you want to make sure you are covered for personal items too. Read the small print before heading off so you are aware of what is covered and what is not, what is required to submit a claim and what to do in the event of an emergency. Always buy insurance before setting out as your options will be more limited and generally quite costly once you've departed from your home country.

Internet

A list of useful websites is given on page 148. Public access to the internet is endemic with cybercafés in both large and small towns. Many hotels and cafés also have Wi-Fi. Speeds and connections are often unreliable, particularly with smart phones and data-hungry applications that place strain on the bandwidth. When using public Wi-Fi, please be considerate of other users.

Language

The official language of Mexico is Spanish. Outside of the main tourist centres, travelling without some knowledge of Spanish is a major hindrance. Adding to the challenges of communication, there are also numerous Mayan languages spoken in southern Mexico.

Media

The influential daily newspapers are: *Excelsior*, *Novedades*, *Uno Más Uno*, *El Universal*, *La Jornada* (www.jornada.unam.mx, more to the left) and *La Prensa* (a popular tabloid, with the largest circulation). There are influential weekly magazines *Proceso* and *Siempre*. *The Miami Herald* is stocked by most news-stands.

Money

US$1 = $15.7. €1 = $17.9. £1 = $25.2 (Jul 2015)

The monetary unit is the Mexican peso, represented by '$' – the dollar sign – which provides great potential for confusion, especially in popular tourist places where prices are higher and often quoted in US dollars (US$). For up-to-the-minute exchange rates visit www.xe.com.

ATMs and credit cards

ATMs are found even in small towns, allowing you to travel without carrying large amounts of cash or TCs. **MasterCard**, **Visa** and **American Express** are widely accepted in Mexico either when paying for goods, withdrawing cash from ATMs (*cajero automático*) or obtaining cash over the counter from banks. There is often a 6% tax on the use of credit cards. For lost or stolen cards call: **MasterCard** T001-800-307-7309; **Visa** T001-800-847-2911.

Currency cards If you don't want to carry lots of cash, prepaid currency cards allow you to preload money from your bank account, fixed at the day's exchange rate. They look like a credit or debit card and are issued by specialist money-changing companies, such as **Travelex** and **Caxton FX**, and the **Post Office**. You can top up and check your balance by phone, online and sometimes by text.

Banks and currency exchange

US dollars cash can be easily changed at banks in all cities and towns and less economically at *casas de cambio*. In any case, they are accepted by most hotels and restaurants in resort towns. Try to carry a mixture of large and small denominations; it can be hard to change notes of US$20 or higher in small villages. While it is possible to change the euro, sterling and other currencies, not all banks or *casas de cambio* will take them.

Transfer If you need to make a transfer ask your bank if they can transfer direct to a Mexican bank without using an intermediary, which usually results in greater delays. Beware of short-changing at all times. **Western Union**, www.westernunion.com, have outlets throughout Mexico but the service is more expensive than a traditional bank wire.

Cost of travelling

Couples and groups will make good savings. A basic bare bones room with a fan and cold water is likely to set you back about US$15 on average. Simple but comfortable rooms with hot water, TV, Wi-Fi, a/c and a good bed start at around US$25. Meals start from US$15 a day for those on tight budgets and activities cost US$30 per day and upwards. Travel is expensive compared to Central America and you should definitely calculate costs into your budget (see Getting around, page 137). An impoverished couple might just survive on US$25-40 per person per day, but US$40-70 is more realistic. Prices are considerably higher in resorts – seek out those places preferred by the locals.

Opening hours

Banks Mon-Fri 0900-1330 (some stay open later), Sat 0900-1230.
Businesses 0900/1000-1300/1400, then 1400/1500-1900 or later. Business hours vary considerably according to the climate and local custom.

Photography

There is a charge of US$3-5 for the use of video cameras at historical sites. For professional camera equipment, including a tripod, the fee is much higher. Never take photos of indigenous people without prior permission.

Police

Probably the best advice with regards the police in Mexico is to have as little to do with them as possible. An exception to this rule are the tourist police, who operate in some of the big cities and resorts, and provide assistance. In general, law enforcement in Mexico is achieved by periodic campaigns, not systematically.

You may be asked for identification at any time and should therefore always have ID on you. If you cannot produce it, you may be jailed. If you are jailed, you should contact your embassy or consulate and take advice. In the event of a vehicle accident in which anyone is injured, all drivers involved are automatically detained until blame has been established, and this does not usually take less than 2 weeks. If a visitor is jailed his or her friends should provide food every day.

The giving and receiving of bribes is not recommended. However, the following advice may prove useful. Never offer a bribe unless you are fully conversant with the customs of the country.

Post

International service has improved and bright red mailboxes, found in many parts of the city, are reliable for letters. Poste Restante (*lista de correos* in Mexico) functions quite reliably, but you may have to ask under each of your names; mail is sent back after 10 days. For more information, see **Correos de México**, www.sepomex.gob.mx.

Public holidays

If any of these holidays falls on a Thursday or a Tuesday, they are usually an excuse for a *puente*, a long weekend (which can have implications for travel, hotel accommodation and services).

National holidays
1 Jan   New Year
5 Feb   Constitution Day
21 Mar   Birthday of Benito Juárez
Mar/Apr   Maundy Thu, Good Fri, Easter Sat
1 May   Labour Day
5 May   Battle of Puebla
1 Sep   El Informe (Presidential Message)
16 Sep   Independence Day
12 Oct   Día de la Raza (Discovery of America)
20 Nov   Día de la Revolución (Revolution Day)
25 Dec   Christmas Day

Religious fiestas
There are more than 5000 religious festivals each year. The most widely celebrated are:
6 Jan Santos Reyes (Three Kings)
10 May Día de las Madres (Mothers' Day)
1-2 Nov Día de los Muertos (All Souls' Day)
12 Dec La Virgen de Guadalupe

Punctuality

Punctuality is more of a concept than a reality in Latin countries. The *mañana* culture reigns supreme and any arrangement to meet at, say 1900, will normally rendezvous somewhere between 2000 and 2100. However, the one time you are late to catch a bus, boat or plane, it will leave on time – the rule is hurry up and wait.

Safety

In recent years, Mexico's feuding drug cartels have been the cause of much unpleasant violence but, despite the horrific scenes reported by the international media, the problem is largely confined to the US border in sketchy barrios you are unlikely to see. Millions of people travel safely to Mexico every year and the Yucatán's homicide rate is actually lower than that in much of rural North America. If you are unfortunate enough to be a victim of crime, it is most likely to be an opportunistic theft, against which you must take the usual sensible precautions. Cars are a prime target; never leave possessions visible inside the car and park in hotel car parks after dark. Avoid travelling at night; if at all possible make journeys in daylight. Avoid lonely beaches, especially if you are a single woman. Other than the tourist police who are helpful, speak some English and who you'll only come across in more touristy areas, it is best to avoid the police if at all possible; they are rarely helpful and tend to make complicated situations even worse. Speaking Spanish is a great asset for avoiding rip-offs targeting gringos, especially short changing and overcharging (both rife). See also Drugs, page 142 and Women travellers, page 149.

On the street and public transport
When you have all your luggage with you at a bus station, be especially careful: don't get into arguments with any locals if you can help it and clip, tie or lock all the items together with a chain or cable if you are waiting for some time, or simply sit on top of your backpack. Take a taxi between airport/bus station/railway station and hotel, if you can afford it. Keep your bags with you in the taxi and pay only when you and your luggage are safely out of the vehicle. Avoid night buses unless essential or until you are comfortable travelling in the area; avoid arriving at night whenever possible; and watch your belongings whether they are stowed inside or outside the cabin (rooftop luggage racks create extra problems, which are sometimes unavoidable – many bus drivers cover rooftop luggage with plastic sheeting, but a waterproof bag or outer sack can be invaluable for protecting your luggage and for stopping someone rummaging through the top of your bag). Major bus lines often issue a luggage ticket when bags are stored in the hold; this is generally a safe system. Finally, be wary of accepting food, drink, sweets or cigarettes from unknown fellow travellers on buses or

trains. Do not take shared taxis with strangers you have met on the bus, no matter how polite or well-dressed.

Scams

A number of distraction techniques such as mustard smearers and paint or shampoo sprayers and strangers' remarks like 'what's that on your shoulder?' or 'have you seen that dirt on your shoe?' are designed to distract you for a few critical moments in which time your bag may be grabbed. Furthermore, supposedly friendly assistance asking if you have dropped money or other items in the street work on the same premise. If someone follows you when you're in the street, let him catch up with you and give him the 'eye'. While you should take local advice about being out at night, do not assume that daytime is any safer. If walking after dark on quiet streets, walk in the road, not on the pavement.

Be wary of 'plain-clothes policemen'; insist on seeing identification and going to the police station by main roads. Do not hand over your identification (or money – which they should not need to see anyway) until you are at the station. On no account take them directly back to your lodgings. Be even more suspicious if they seek confirmation of their status from a passer-by. If someone implies they are asking for a bribe, insist on a receipt. If attacked, remember your assailants may well be armed, and try not to resist.

It is best, if you can trust your hotel, to leave any valuables you don't need in a safe-deposit. Always keep an inventory of what you have deposited. If you don't trust the hotel, lock everything in your pack and secure that in your room. If you do lose valuables, you will need to report the incident to the police for insurance purposes.

Student and teacher travellers

If you are in full-time education you will be entitled to an **International Student Identity Card (ISIC)**, which is distributed by student travel offices and travel agencies in over 100 countries. ISIC gives you special prices on all forms of transport (air, sea, rail, etc), and a variety of other concessions and services. Contact the **International Student Travel Confederation (ISTC)**, T+31-20-421 2800, www.isic.org. Student cards must carry a photograph if they are to be of any use for discounts in Latin America. The ISIC website provides a list of card-issuing offices around the world. Teachers may want to take an **International Teacher Identity Card (ITIC)** distributed by ISTC (above), as discounts are often extended to teachers. Note that only national Mexican student cards permit free entry to museums, archaeological sites, etc.

Tax

Impuesto al Valor Agregado (IVA) applies to most goods and services at 16%. Hotel tax is 3-5%. For departure tax, see page 135.

Telephone

Country code T+52
Operator T020; international operator T090; directory enquiries T040.
Many of the telecommunications networks have been privatized and prices have fallen considerably. International telecom charge cards are useful and available from most countries; obtain details before leaving home.

For the US AT&T's **USA Direct**, **Sprint** and **MCI** are all available for calls to the US. It is much cheaper than operator-assisted calls. Internet calls (eg via **Skype**, **Whatsapp** and **Viber**) are also possible if you have access to Wi-Fi.

Using a mobile in Mexico is very expensive and may not be worth your while. Mobile phone calls will be cheaper if you buy a SIM card for the local network; in-country calls are likely to be considerably cheaper than using your home-based account. The initial cost of the SIM is getting more affordable (as little as US$3), but check the cost of calls. Also bear in mind that the number you use at home will not work. Some networks, eg **O2**, provide an app so you can use the time on your contract if you access the app via Wi-Fi.

Most destinations have a 7-digit number and 3-digit regional code (Mexico City is an exception). The format of a number, depending on the type of call, should be as follows: **local** 7- or 8-digit phone number; **regional** long-distance access code (01) + regional code (2- or 3-digit code) + 7- or 8-digit number; **international** international direct-dialling code + country code + regional code + 7- or 8-digit number. Most public phones take phone cards only (**Ladatel**) costing 30 or 50 pesos from shops and news kiosks everywhere. Reverse-charge (collect) calls can be made from any blue public phone; say you want to *llamar por cobrar*. Pre-paid phone cards are expensive for international calls. Of other pre-paid cards, the best value are **Ekofon**, www.ekofon.com.

Time

Southern Mexico is in Central Standard Time (CST), 6 hrs behind GMT. Daylight Saving Time runs from the 1st Sun in Apr to the last Sun in Oct (when it is 5 hrs behind GMT).

Tipping

Normally 10-15%; the equivalent of US$0.25 per bag for porters, the equivalent of US$0.20 for bell boys and nothing for a taxi driver unless some kind of exceptional service has been provided.

Tourist information

Tourist offices are listed throughout the text. In Europe, information is available in several different languages by calling T00-800-1111- 2266. In North America call T1-800-446-3942.

Useful websites
Some of the reliable, informative and useful websites that have been round for a while include:
www.mexconnect.com General information.
www.mexperience.com Well-constructed site updated daily, with current affairs, feature articles and advice on travel in Mexico. Look out for the forum where comments from fellow travellers are exchanged.
www.sectur.gob.mx Tourism Secretariat's site, with less glossy links but equally comprehensive information.
www.visitmexico.com Mexico Tourist Board site, a comprehensive multilingual site with information on the entire country.

Visas and immigration

Virtually all international travellers require a passport to enter Mexico. Upon entry you will be issued a tourist card known as a **Forma Migratoria Múltiple**

(FMM), valid for up to 180 days. The card comes with a fee,

The **Derecho de No Migrante (DNI)** costs approximately US$22, which you must pay upon exit, or if you prefer, upon entry – be sure to get a stamp and keep all receipts. If arriving in Cancún or Mexico City, the DNI is often included in airfares. Nonetheless, when exiting at land borders, you must present evidence of this to avoid being charged a 2nd time (this issue has been frequently reported at the Mexico–Belize border). On your plane ticket, the DNI is indicated by the code 'UK' – print the page and highlight it. Note your FMM must surrendered when leaving the country to avoid problems later. If you are in Mexico for 7 days or less and you return to your country of origin, you are exempt from the DNI.

If your stamp bears less than 180 days, you can extend it up to the limit at any **National Institute of Migration** office; you can find details at www.inm.gob.mx. To renew a tourist card by leaving the country, you must stay outside Mexico for at least 72 hrs.

Take TCs or a credit card as proof of finance. At the border crossings with Belize and Guatemala, you may be refused entry into Mexico if you have less than US$200 (or US$350 for each month of intended stay, up to a maximum of 180 days). Likewise, if you are carrying more than US$10,000 in cash or TCs, you must declare it.

If a person under 18 is travelling alone or with one parent, both parents' consent is required, certified by a notary or authorized by a consulate. A divorced parent must be able to show custody of a child. (These requirements are not always checked by immigration authorities and do not apply to all nationalities.) Further details are available from any Mexican consulate.

Weights and measures

The metric system is used.

Women travellers

Some women experience problems, whether accompanied or not; others encounter no difficulties at all. Unaccompanied Western women will at times be subject to close scrutiny and exceptional curiosity. Don't be unduly scared. Simply be prepared and try not to over-react. When you set out, err on the side of caution until your instincts have adjusted to the new culture. Women travelling alone could consider taking a wedding ring to prevent being hassled. To help minimize unwanted attention, consider your clothing choices. Do not feel bad about showing offence. When accepting an invitation, make sure that someone else knows the address you are going to and the time you left. Ask if you can bring a friend (even if you do not intend to do so). A good rule is always to act with confidence, as though you know where you are going, even if you do not. Someone who looks lost is more likely to attract unwanted attention. Do not disclose to strangers where you are staying.

Index

→ *Entries in* **bold** *refer to maps*

A

Acanceh 89
accommodation
   price codes 16
Aguilar, Gerónimo de 40
Aké 94

B

Bacalar 68
Balankanché Caves 98
Banco Chinchorro 64
Becal 114
Becán 119
books
border crossings
   Control Agreement (CA-4) 138
   Mexico–Belize 139

C

Cabo Catoche 40
Calakmul 118
Calderitas 67
Campeche 106, **107**
Campeche State 105
Cancún 24, **25**
Captain Enciso y Valdivia 40
Caste War 66
Castillo Real 51
Celestún 78
Cenote Azul 68
Cenote Dzitnup 101
Cenote X-Kekén 101
Cenote Xlaca 79
Cenote Zací 101
Cenotillo 94
Chablekal 79
Chacmultún 90
Champotón 115
Chelem 78
Chetumal 66, **69**
Chicanná 119
Chichén Itzá 95
Chicxulub 78
children, travelling with 141
Chumayel 89
Chunyaxché 59
Ciudad del Carmen 115
Cobá 58
Cortés, Hernán 116
Cozumel 49, **50**
culture 130
currency cards 144
customs 141

D

disabled travellers 141
diving
   cenotes 63
dress code 142
drugs 142
duty free 141
Dzab-Náh 89
Dzibalchén 114
Dzibanché 68
Dzibilchaltún 79
Dzibilnocac 114
Dzitnup 101

E

Edzná 113
Ek-Balam 101
El Cedral 52
electricity 142
El Gran Museo del Mundo Maya 77
embassies and consulates 142
Escárcega 118

F

Felipe Carrillo Puerto 64
gay and lesbian travellers 142
Grutas de Balankanché 98
Gulf coast 115

H

hammocks 31
health 142
Hernández de Córdoba, Francisco 108, 115
Hochob 114
Hoctún 94
Hopelchén 114
Hormiguero 120
hotels
   price codes 16

I

Ichpaatun 68
insurance 143
internet 143
Isla Contoy 39
Isla Holbox 39
Isla Mujeres 33, **33**
Izamal 94

K

Kabah 91
Kanasín 89
Knichná 68
Kohunlich 68

L

Labná 92
Lago Macanxoc 58
Laguna de los Milagros 68
La Malinche 116
Landa, Diego de 94
land and environment
language 143
La Unión 94
Lerma 109
Loltún 90

M

Majahual 64
Malinche, La 116
Mama 89
Maní 89
Maxcanú 79
Mayapán 89
media 144
Mérida 74, **75**
money 144
Muyil 59

N

national holidays 145
Nohochmul 68

O

opening hours 145
Oxcutzcab 90
Oxkintoc 79
Oxtancah 68

P

Palmara 68
Panama hats 114
photography 145
Playa del Carmen 43, **44**
police 145
post 145
price codes 16
Progreso 78
public holidays 145
Puerto Morelos 43
Puerto Yucalpetén 78
punctuality 146
Puuc Route 91

Q

Quintana Roo State 23

R

restaurants 18
   price codes 16
Río Bec 120
Río Lagartos 102

S

safety 146
San Bernardo 79
San Gervasio 51
Santa Lucía 40
San Miguel de Cozumel 49, **52**
Sayil 92
Seybaplaya 115
Sian Ka'an Biosphere Reserve 59
Sihoplaya 115
student travellers 147

T

tax 147
Teabo 89
Tecoh 89
Tekax 90
Tekit 89
Telchaquillo 89
telephone 147
tequila 19
Ticul 90
Tipikal 89
tipping 148
Tizimín 102
tourist information 148
transport 135
Tulum 56, **57**

U

Ucil 94
Ucum 68
Umán 79
Uxmal 92

V

Valladolid 100, **100**
visas and immigration 148

W

weather 10
women travellers 149

X

Xlapak 92
Xpujil 119

Y

Yucatán State 73

Credits

Footprint credits

Editor: Nicola Gibbs
Production and layout: Patrick Dawson
Maps: Kevin Feeney
Colour section: Angus Dawson

Publisher: Patrick Dawson
Managing Editor: Felicity Laughton
Administration: Elizabeth Taylor
Advertising sales and marketing:
John Sadler, Kirsty Holmes
Business Development: Debbie Wylde

Photography credits

Front cover: cristovao/Shutterstock.com
Back cover: Top: alessandro0770/Shutterstock.com. Bottom: Victor Torres/Shutterstock.com.

Colour section
Inside front cover: Gerald Marella/Shutterstock.com, Vadim Petrakov/Shutterstock.com, francesco de marco/Shutterstock.com, Elzbieta Sekowska/Shutterstock.com. **Page 1**: milosk50/Shutterstock.com. **Page 2**: Polly Dawson/Shutterstock.com. **Page 4**: Eddy Galeotti/Shutterstock.com. **Page 5**: Luis Javier Sandoval Alvarado/SuperStock, Gerald Marella/Shutterstock.com, Jose Ignacio Soto/Shutterstock.com. **Page 6**: Photononstop/SuperStock. **Page 7**: Christopher Russell/Dreamstime.com. **Page 8**: Noradoa/Shutterstock.com. **Duotone Page 20**: Victor Torres/Shutterstock.com.

Printed in Spain by GraphyCems

Publishing information

Footprint Cancún & Yucatán Peninsula
3rd edition
© Footprint Handbooks Ltd
September 2015

ISBN: 978 1 910120 50 7
CIP DATA: A catalogue record for this book is available from the British Library

® Footprint Handbooks and the Footprint mark are a registered trademark of Footprint Handbooks Ltd

Published by Footprint
6 Riverside Court
Lower Bristol Road
Bath BA2 3DZ, UK
T +44 (0)1225 469141
F +44 (0)1225 469461
footprinttravelguides.com

Distributed in the USA by
National Book Network, Inc.

Every effort has been made to ensure that the facts in this guidebook are accurate. However, travellers should still obtain advice from consulates, airlines, etc about travel and visa requirements before travelling. The authors and publishers cannot accept responsibility for any loss, injury or inconvenience however caused.

All rights reserved. No part of this publication may be reproduced, stored in a retrieval system, or transmitted, in any form or by any means, electronic, mechanical, photocopying, recording, or otherwise without the prior permission of Footprint Handbooks Ltd.